GHANA

Marxist Regimes Series

Series editor: Bogdan Szajkowski,
Department of Sociology, University College,
Cardiff

Afghanistan Bhabani Sen Gupta
Ethiopia Peter Schwab
Ghana Donald I. Ray
Grenada Tony Thorndike
Guyana Colin Baber and Henry B. Jeffrey
Hungary Hans-Georg Heinrich
Romania Michael Shafir
Soviet Union Ronald J. Hill

Further Titles

Albania
Angola
Benin and The Congo
Bulgaria
Cape Verde, São Tomé and Príncipe
China
Cuba
Czechoslovakia
German Democratic Republic
Guinea-Bissau
Kampuchea
Democratic People's Republic of Korea
Laos
Madagascar
Mongolia
Mozambique
Nicaragua
Poland
Surinam
Vietnam
People's Democratic Republic of Yemen
Yugoslavia
Zimbabwe
Marxist State Governments in India
Marxist Local Governments in Western Europe and Japan
The Diversification of Communism
Comparative Analysis
Cumulative Index

GHANA

Politics, Economics and Society

Donald I. Ray

Frances Pinter (Publishers), London

Lynne Rienner Publishers, Inc., Boulder

© Donald I. Ray 1986

First published in Great Britain in 1986 by
Frances Pinter (Publishers) Limited
25 Floral Street, London WC2E 9DS

First published in the United States of America by
Lynne Rienner Publishers, Inc.
948 North Street
Boulder, Colorado 80302

British Library Cataloguing in Publication Data
Ray, Donald I.
    Ghana: politics, economics and society.—
    (Marxist regime series)
    1. Ghana—Politics and government
    I. Title   II. Series
    320.9667   JQ3028
    ISBN 0-86187-475-1
    ISBN 0-86187-476-5 Pbk

Library of Congress Cataloging in Publication Data
Ray, Donald Iain, 1949–
    Ghana: politics, economics, and society.
    (Marxist regimes)
    Bibliography: p.
    Includes index.
    1. Ghana—Politics and government.   2. Ghana—
    Economic conditions.   3. Ghana—Social conditions.
    I. Title.   II. Series.
    DT510.62.R39   1986   966.7 '05   86-10200
    ISBN 0-931477-62-X (Rienner)
    ISBN 0-931477-61-1 (Rienner: pbk.)

Typeset by Joshua Associates Limited, Oxford
Printed by SRP Limited, Exeter

Editor's Preface

Studies of social, political and economic structures of African societies have on the whole been marked by the strengths and weaknesses of distinctly partisan approaches to that continent's complex problems. To many writers these problems seem almost insurmountable and their studies often appear to convert as well as to reassure the converted, rather than to convince the reader, and supply evidence to the student to assess the available options. This, the first comprehensive book on the politics, economics and society of the Marxist regime in Ghana, bridges the gap that has inhibited writers from exploring the Marxist option in a scholarly and non-partisan way.

The example and experience of the Marxist regime in Ghana is particularly illuminating in the wider context of the study of Marxist polities. Such studies have commonly been equated with the study of communist political systems. For many years it was not difficult to distinguish the eight regimes in Eastern Europe and four in Asia which resoundingly claimed adherence to the tenets of Marxism and more particularly to their Soviet interpretation—Marxism-Leninism. These regimes, variously called 'People's Republic', 'People's Democratic Republic', or 'Democratic Republic', claimed to have derived their inspiration from the Soviet Union to which, indeed, in the overwhelming number of cases they owed their establishment.

To many scholars and analysts these regimes represented a multiplication of and geographical extension of the 'Soviet model' and consequently of the Soviet sphere of influence. Although there were clearly substantial similarities between the Soviet Union and the people's democracies, especially in the initial phases of their development, these were often overstressed at the expense of noticing the differences between these political systems.

It took a few years for scholars to realize that generalizing the particular, i.e. applying the Soviet experience to other states ruled by elites which claimed to be guided by 'scientific socialism', was not good enough. The relative simplicity of the assumption of a cohesive communist bloc was questioned after the expulsion of Yugoslavia from the Communist Information Bureau in 1948 and in particular after the workers' riots in Poznań in 1956 and the Hungarian revolution of the same year. By the mid-1960s, the totalitarian model of communist politics, which until then had been very much in force, began to crumble. As some of these regimes articulated demands for a distinctive path of socialist development, many specialists studying these systems began to notice that the cohesiveness of the communist bloc was less apparent than had been claimed before.

Also by the mid-1960s, in the newly independent African states 'democratic' multi-party states were turning into one-party states or military dictatorships, thus questioning the inherent superiority of liberal democracy, capitalism and the values that went with it. Scholars now began to ponder on the simple contrast between multi-party democracy and a one-party totalitarian rule that had satisfied an earlier generation.

More importantly, however, by the beginning of that decade Cuba had a revolution without Soviet help, a revolution which subsequently became to many political elites in the Third World not only an inspiration but a clear military, political and ideological example to follow. Apart from its romantic appeal, to many nationalist movements the Cuban revolution also demonstrated a novel way of conducting and winning a nationalist, anti-imperialist war and accepting Marxism as the state ideology without a vanguard communist party. The Cuban precedent was subsequently followed in one respect or another by scores of regimes in the Third World who used the adoption of 'scientific socialism' tied to the tradition of Marxist thought as a form of mobilization, legitimation or association with the prestigious symbols and powerful high-status regimes such as the Soviet Union, China, Cuba and Vietnam.

Despite all these changes the study of Marxist regimes remains in its infancy and continues to be hampered by constant and not always pertinent comparison with the Soviet Union, thus somewhat blurring the important underlying common theme—the 'scientific theory' of the laws of development of human society and human history. This doctrine is claimed by the leadership of these regimes to consist of the discovery of objective causal relationships; it is used to analyse the contradictions which arise between goals and actuality in the pursuit of a common destiny. Thus the political elites of these countries have been and continue to be influenced in both their ideology and their political practice by Marxism more than any other current of social thought and political practice.

The growth in the number and global significance, as well as the ideological political and economic impact, of Marxist regimes has presented scholars and students with an increasing challenge. In meeting this challenge, social scientists on both sides of the political divide have put forward a dazzling profusion of terms, models, programmes and varieties of interpretation. It is against the background of this profusion that the present comprehensive series on Marxist regimes is offered.

This collection of monographs is envisaged as a series of multi-disciplinary textbooks on the governments, politics, economics and society of these countries. Each of the monographs was prepared by a specialist on the country concerned. Thus, over fifty scholars from all over the world have contributed monographs which were based on first-hand knowledge. The geographical diversity of the authors, combined with the fact that as a group they represent many disciplines of social science, gives their individual analyses and the series as a whole an additional dimension.

Each of the scholars who contributed to this series was asked to analyse such topics as the political culture, the governmental structure, the ruling party, other mass organizations, party-state relations, the policy process, the economy, domestic and foreign relations together with any features peculiar to the country under discussion.

This series does not aim at assigning authenticity or authority to any single one of the political systems included in it. It shows that depending on a variety of historical, cultural, ethnic and political factors, the pursuit of goals derived from the tenets of Marxism has produced different political forms at different times and in different places. It also illustrates the rich diversity among these societies, where attempts to achieve a synthesis between goals derived from Marxism on the one hand, and national realities on the other, have often meant distinctive approaches and solutions to the problems of social, political and economic development.

University College   *Bogdan Szajkowski*
Cardiff

To my Father

Contents

List of Illustrations and Tables

Map

Figures

Tables

Preface

To Those Who Stayed, From One Who Came

Ghana under the Provisional National Defence Council (PNDC) is surrounded by a great deal of mystery and confusion. If the diplomatic community in Ghana is agreed upon anything, it is on how little understood the Ghanaian revolution really is. One senior Soviet scholar visiting Ghana was asked to characterize the revolution. When pressed, he described it as 'unique'. Participants in the revolution sometimes seem to be describing completely different countries. As Professor Szajkowski has noted, the pattern of social transformation of this century clearly dictates an intellectual need to break away from the old categories and preconceptions. Ghana certainly underlines the point.

A unique and unexpected conjunction of forces have produced this Ghanaian revolution. Ghana's future depends very much on the degree to which the PNDC succeeds in implementing its programme.

I am most grateful to those who helped me in the writing of this book. Bogdan Szajkowski, the General Editor of this series, Heather Bliss and Peter Moulson of Frances Pinter provided encouragement. Their understanding after my father's sudden death has been greatly appreciated. Tareq and Jackie Ismael have been a constant source of friendship and intellectual stimulation. Peter and Ama Shinnie convinced me that I had to go to Ghana: I too have fallen in love with the country. I owe a special debt of friendship to K. and I., H. and H.G. and the family. Sherry Slater, especially and Geanine Robey and Debra Carnet provided important research assistance for this project. Others in Calgary who helped were Rhys Williams, Judy Pelchat and ILLO, Trust Accounting, Margaret Reed, Mary Gray, Cecile Calverley and Ella Wensel. Judi Powell did a magnificent job of typing the manuscript. The Department of Political Science provided the necessary ongoing administrative support. The University of Calgary approved the sabbatical during which I wrote the book and I am grateful for this assistance.

The research was funded by the Social Sciences and Humanities Research Council of Canada, the University of Calgary's Operating Grants, and the Government of Canada's SEED programme. Pat Evans, Hilda Nantais, Ruth Nymand, Pat Aldridge and Trish Holmgren guided me through the various mysteries of funding: I am grateful to them also.

It is impossible to adequately acknowledge my colleagues and friends in Ghana. So often in the writing of this book, I found myself saying, 'Ah, but here my discussion/interview with X was so important'. It does not seem fair that I cannot freely acknowledge these debts; nevertheless, the pledge that I signed for the university's ethics committee binds me not to reveal many of my sources. All I can ask is that those concerned will understand. Consequently, in many cases only documentary sources have been cited. However, I can express my considerable gratitude to my colleagues at the University of Ghana for their legendary hospitality and intellectual stimulation. I owe a special debt to the Department of Political Science and to its Head, Dr Kwame Ninsin, for so kindly being my hosts.

I dedicate this book to my father (Don), my mother (Honey), my wife (Rosemary) and our children (Michael, Matthew and Jenny).

Donald I. Ray

Department of Political Science,
University of Calgary

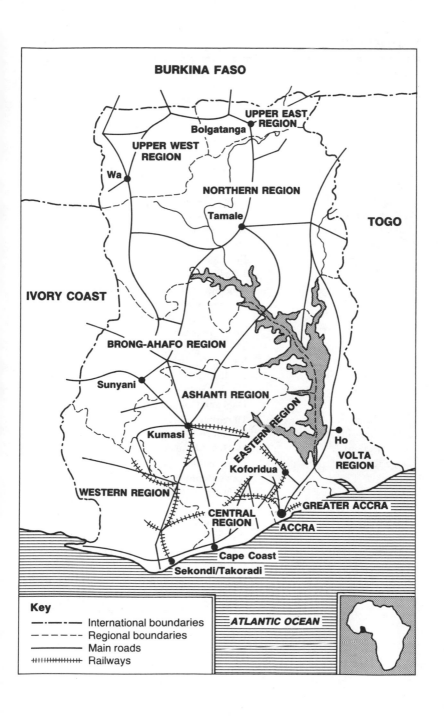

BURKINA FASO

UPPER EAST REGION

Bolgatanga

UPPER WEST REGION

Wa

NORTHERN REGION

Tamale

TOGO

IVORY COAST

BRONG-AHAFO REGION

Sunyani

ASHANTI REGION

EASTERN REGION

Kumasi

Koforidua

Ho

VOLTA REGION

WESTERN REGION

CENTRAL REGION

GREATER ACCRA

ACCRA

Cape Coast

Sekondi/Takoradi

Key
—·—·— International boundaries
— — — Regional boundaries
———— Main roads
+++++++++ Railways

ATLANTIC OCEAN

Basic Data

Official name	Republic of Ghana
Population	12,205,574
Population density	51 per sq. km.
Population growth (% p.a.)	2.6 (1970–84)
Urban population (%)	31.3 (1984)
Total labour force	3.4 million (1983)
Life expectancy	55.6 (1984)
Infant death rate (per 1,000)	76.3 (1984)
Child death rate per (1,000)	19 (1980)
Ethnic groups	By language group in north: Mole-Dagbane 14%; Gurma 4%; Grusi 2%; others 10%. By language group in the south: Akan 44%; Ewe 13%; Ga Adangbe 8%; Guan 4%; Central Togo 1%; others mostly British
Capital	Accra (pop. 636,067)
Land area	239,460 sq. km., of which 19% arable, 60% forests, 21% other
Official language	English
Other main languages	South: Twi, Fante, Ewe, Ga, Nzema. North: Dagbani, Gonja, Hausa
Administrative divisions	10 regions
Membership of international organizations	UN since 1957, Commonwealth since 1957, OAU since 1963
Foreign relations	Diplomatic and consular relations with 37 states. Representatives of 44 countries residing in Accra (1986).
Political structure	
Constitution	Provisional National Defence Council (Establishment) Proclamation, 1981 (11 January 1982); PNDC laws; the unsuspended parts of the 1979 Third Republic Constitution; the relevant acts of the civilian governments (1957–66, 1969–72, 1979–81) and the relevant decrees of the military governments (1966–9, 1972–5, 1975–8, 1978–9, 1979) and unwritten customary provisions.
Highest legislative body	None

Highest executive body	Provisional National Defence Council (PNDC)
Prime Minister (PNDC Co-ordinating Secretary)	P. V. Obeng
President (Chairman of the PNDC)	Jerry John Rawlings
Ruling party	None as such, but the most influential movements were the New Democratic Movement and, until November 1982, the June Fourth Movement. Defence Committees played a quasi-party role.
Party membership	None as such. Membership totals of the movements are uncertain, though probably 10–30,000
Growth indicators (% p.a.)	
GNP	−1% (1960–80), 0.7% (1983), 5.5% (1984)
GDP	2.1% (1960–70), −0.1% (1970–80)
Industry	
Total	−1.2% (1970–80)
Manufacturing	−2.9% (1970–80)
Agriculture	−1.2% (1970–80)
Services	1% (1970–80)
Trade and Balance of payments	
Exports	US$878.2 million (1982) f.o.b.
Imports	US$1,83.7 million (1982) c.i.f.
Exports as % of GNP	3.1% (1981)
Main exports	Cocoa, tropical hardwoods, gold, diamonds, manganese, bauxite, aluminium, oil, electricity from the Lake Volta complex
Main imports	Oil, machinery and transportation equipment, manufactured products, foodstuffs.
Destination of exports (%)	Socialist industrial (15), industrial non-socialist (70), developing (15)
Main trading partners	
Exports (%)	USSR (8), US (26), UK (13), Japan (12), West Germany (9), Netherlands (3), Other (29)
Imports (%)	US (21), US (14), Nigeria (13), West Germany (10), Other (42)
Foreign debt	US$1,708.2 million (1985)
Foreign aid	US$175.2 million, excluding military aid (1981)
Main natural resources	Cocoa, tropical hardwoods, bauxite, gold, diamonds, manganese (also some oil and gas)

Food self-sufficiency	Food production per capita in 1980-2 was 72% of that in 1969-71 (World Bank, 1984). Shortage of rice (since 1979), wheat (since 1971) and coarse grains (since 1971). According to the World Bank (1984), consumption is growing at 2.6%, while agricultural production has been declining, at −0.2%.
Armed forces	15,600 (there are also 10,000 police)

Education and health

School system	Thirteen years (1983)
Primary school enrolment	69% of school-age children enrolled (1979)
Secondary school enrolment	36% of age-group enrolled (1979)
Higher education	1% of age group 20–24 enrolled (1979)— University of Ghana (Accra), University of Cape Coast, University of Science and Technology (Kumasi)
Adult literacy (%)	30.2 (1970)
Population per hospital bed	665 (1979)
Population per physician	7,245 (1979)

Economy

GNP	US$13.7 billion (1980)
GNP per capita	US$356 (1982 est.)
GDP by %	Agriculture (51), industry (8), services (41) (1982)
Budget (expenditure)	US$915.3 million
Defence expenditure as % of state budget	5%
Monetary unit	Cedi ¢90 = US$1 (1986)
Main crops	Cocoa, cassava, yams, plantains, corn (maize), sorghum, millet, peanuts, fruit, coconuts, palm oil, palm kernels, coffee, shea nuts, rubber, cattle, goats, fish
Land tenure	Traditional usufructure and private owner-ship
Main religions (%)	Christianity 43; Islam 12; various indigenous 38; no religious affiliation 7

Transport

Rail network	953 km
Road network	32,000 km.

Population Forecasting

The following data projections were produced by Poptran, Cardiff University Population Centre, from United Nations Assessment Data published in 1980. These projections have been reproduced here to provide some comparative indices with other countries covered by the Marxist Regime Series.

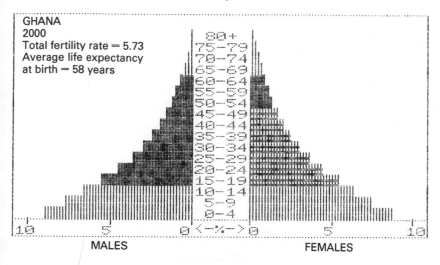

GHANA
2000
Total fertility rate = 5.73
Average life expectancy
at birth = 58 years

MALES   FEMALES

Projected Data for Ghana 2000

Total population ('000)	22,346
Males ('000)	11,096
Females ('000)	11,250
Total fertility rate	5.73
Life expectancy (male)	56.3 years
Life expectancy (female)	60.0 years
Crude birth rate	42.1
Crude death rate	10.5
Annual growth rate	3.16%
Under 15s	45.98%
Over 65s	2.84%
Woman aged 15–49	22.67%
Doubling time	22 years
Population density	94 per sq. km.
Urban population	51.2%

List of Abbreviations

AC	*Africa Confidential*
ADB	Africa Development Bank
AFRC	Armed Forces Revolutionary Council
AI	Amnesty International
AWAG	All Women's Association of Ghana
AYB	African Youth Brigade
AYC	African Youth Command
CVC	Citizens Vetting Committee
CDR	Committe for the Defence of the Revolution
CPP	Convention People's Party
CPSU	Communist Party of the Soviet Union
DG	*Daily Graphic*
DYLG	Democratic Youth League of Ghana
ECA	Economic Committee for Africa (UN)
ECOWAS	Economic Community of West African States
FAO	Food and Agriculture Organization (UN)
GBC	Ghana Broadcasting Corporation
GIHOC	Ghana Industrial Holding Corporation
GNP	Gross National Product
GDP	Gross Domestic Product
GT	*Ghanaian Times*
IBRD	International Bank for Reconstruction and Development ('World Bank')
IDA	International Development Association (see IBRD)
IMC	Interim Management Committee
IMF	International Monetary Fund
JCC	Joint Consultative Committee
JFM	June Fourth Movement
KNRG	Kwame Nkrumah Revolutionary Guards
MONAS	Movement on National Affairs
MOPAD	Movement for Peace and Democracy
NAM	Non-Aligned Movement
NDC	National Defence Committee
NEP	New Economic Policy
NDM	New Democratic Movement
NIC	National Investigations Committee
NLC	National Liberation Council.
NRC	National Redemption Council

NUGS	National Union of Ghana Students
NYOC	National Youth Organizing Commission
OAU	Organization for African Unity
PDC	People's Defence Committee
PDG	*People's Daily Graphic*
PNDC	Provisional National Defence Council
PNP	People's National Party
PRLG	People's Revolutionary League of Ghana
PRP	People's Revolutionary Party
RDC	Regional Defence Committee
SMC	Supreme Military Council
SRYLOG	Socialist Revolutionary Youth League of Ghana
SWAPO	South West African People's Organization (Namibia)
UGCC	United Gold Coast Convention
UN	United Nations
UNESCO	United Nations Educational, Scientific and Cultural Organization
UST	University of Science and Technology
WA	*West Africa*
WDC	Workers' Defence Committee
WHO	World Health Organization

1 History, Political Traditions and Social Structure

Geographical, Economic and Social Setting

The beauty of Ghana's scenery lies not in any spectacular ranges of mountains—most of Ghana is low-lying—but rather in the dramatic variations in vegetation, the surprise with which the traveller meets the hills in certain parts of the country, the sea coast, the many rivers and streams and the giant, man-made Lake Volta that seems to bisect the country. The northern shore of Lake Volta and the connecting Black Volta river provide a convenient dividing line for the country into its northern and southern sections.

Landing on the sandy, coconut tree dotted beach of Accra, the visitor sees the waves roll in across the South Atlantic from Brazil. Proceeding inland, the traveller passes first through the bustling capital city of Accra, next through shrub and open plains, and then the tropical rainforest of the southern centre. Emerging from the forest in a northerly direction, the visitor notes how the vegetation gradually changes in response to the increasing dryness. The first 'Fan' palms can be seen. The bush gives way to savannah and open plains. Much of the openness can be attributed to human agency—farming and firewood cutting. The visitor will see, interspersed among these features, the lines of ridges and hills, especially to the south and east, as well as Lake Volta which impedes both north–south and east–west travel. Ghana's climate ranges from humid-tropical in the south to semi-arid in the north.

Ghana is on the Atlantic coast of West Africa, and shares its 2,285 km. (1,420 mls.) of boundary with Ivory Coast to the west, Burkina Faso (formerly Upper Volta) to the north and Togo to the east, as well as having 572 km. (355 mls.) of coastline. As the crow flies from north to south, Ghana extends 840 km. (522 mls.) in length. Ghana's total land area of 239,460 sq. km. (92,100 sq. mls.) is nearly equal to that of the United Kingdom and West Germany: Canada is forty-two times the size of Ghana, the United States is thirty-nine times as large, while the Soviet Union dwarfs Ghana, being ninety-four times as large.

Ghana's economy has been dominated by agriculture and mining but has also had an important component of import-substitution manufacturing. Ghana's main exports are cocoa (which accounted for 60 per cent of total exports in 1984), timber, gold and bauxite. Ghana once produced nearly one-third of the world crop of cocoa but this has drastically fallen, as has food production. Droughts, forest and bush fires, inadequate compensation to producers from government buyers, smuggling of produce to neighbouring countries to take advantage of higher prices, and other factors have all contributed to lower production, both real and apparent.

Nkrumah's heritage of a greatly expanded light manufacturing sector has been vulnerable to shortages of foreign exchange. Some 95 per cent of raw materials for the import-substitution industries of tyre manufacturing, bus and truck assembly, oil refining, textiles, steel, batteries and other consumer goods have to be imported. The main imports are oil (which cost Ghana 18 per cent of its foreign exchange earnings in 1984), machinery and transportation equipment, components for use in Ghana's import-substitution industries, manufactured products and foodstuffs.

The United States, the United Kingdom, West Germany, Japan, Nigeria and the Soviet Union have been Ghana's major trading partners. There has been a gradual shift in trade away from countries with 'industrial market economies' (i.e. industrialized capitalist) and towards those 'non-market industrial economies', most notably the Soviet Union, as well as those with 'developing economies'.

The continuing imbalance in trade has been reflected in the growing problem of Ghana's status as a debtor nation. By 1980 6 per cent of Ghana's foreign exchange earnings from exports were being consumed by foreign debt servicing. Yet in comparison to much-touted success stories such as Ivory Coast, Ghana's per capita foreign debt was less than one-fifth that of its neighbour.

Communications facilities have mainly been concentrated in the south. Railways connect the southern port of Takoradi with the southern cities of Accra and Kumasi, a collecting-point for the cocoa and gold. The road network is adequate in the south and sparse in the north. By 1983 many of the roads and railways were in poor or very poor condition. The road from Kumasi to the north had become so badly eroded that many truckers refused to use the route because of the wear and tear on their vehicles. By 1984, the PNDC was receiving loans from the World Bank/IMF to repair the roads and railways. The inland shipping route on Lake Volta has been hindered by the lowering of water levels, caused by drought, and by the neglect of equipment during previous administrations. International air traffic has been operated on a regular basis, domestic air travel less so. Telephone and mail services have come to reflect Ghana's economic problems. Ghana has had and continues to have an active media, much of which has been state-owned.

While Ghana's economy recorded growth in the 1950s and part of the 1960s, the 1970s was a decade with very severe economic problems. This was especially so in the aftermath of the drastic price increases for petroleum products in 1973 which consumed much of Ghana's foreign exchange and in the aftermath of the 1966 fall of Kwame Nkrumah's elected government to a rapid succession of military and civilian governments. The military regime of General Achaempong (1972-8) marked an excess of military malfeasance by those officers who looted not only the national territory, but indeed the entire economy (Oquaye, 1980).

The growth of the economic crisis of the post-Nkrumah but pre-PNDC Ghana can be measured in several ways. Inflation was rampant. In six years (1975-80) the wholesale price index rose nearly 800 per cent. In seven years (1975-81) the consumer price index increased by nearly 3,000 per cent. In four years (1978-81) the money supply more than doubled. As a result of de facto devaluation of the Ghana Cedi between 1978 and 1981, the average person paid nearly twice as much for imported goods.

However, the real impact of the economic crisis, caused by both internal and external factors, was not felt until after the pre-revolutionary governments had fallen from power. The Revolution of December 31st 1981, led by the PNDC, was thus saddled with daunting economic problems and a need for drastic solutions. In four years, as the PNDC attempted to resuscitate the Ghanaian economy by getting foreign loans,

Ghanaians saw imported goods rise to nearly twenty times their 1981 level because of the necessary devaluations.

Between 1960 and 1984 Ghana's population nearly doubled, to 12,205,574. Not only has there been a growth in absolute numbers, but the population has been concentrated in the urban areas. Urban dwellers increased from 28.9 per cent of the population in 1970, to 31.3 per cent in 1984. At the same time, the number of towns with over 5,000 people more than doubled, to 199, and two cities, Accra and Kumasi, topped the 500,000 mark. The vast majority of the towns are located in the south, but two-thirds of all Ghanaians still live in the countryside.

Independence has brought very tangible results to Ghana. Life expectancy increased from 40 years in 1960 to 55.2 years in 1984. More children have lived as a result of the funds poured into social welfare by the nationalist progressive movement of Kwame Nkrumah (1951–66).

There is a certain mythology in Ghana to the effect that northern Ghanaians are all Muslim and southerners are all Christian. This is a distortion. Certainly it is true that most of the 43 per cent of Ghanaians who are Christian live in the south and that many of Ghana's 12 per cent who are Muslim live in the north, but there are sizeable numbers who do not live in their 'traditional' areas. Moreover, 38 per cent of Ghanaians have indigenous religions and 7 per cent have no stated religious affiliation. Ghana is a country which takes the non-material very seriously. Religious songs and slogans are to be found everywhere: on the radio, on the streets, on paths and on trucks. According to several religious sources, little of the theology of social justice has yet permeated the religions of Ghana.

There is no political polarization along religious lines, but there has been a religious aspect to the exercise of power in some cases. The Gonja aristocracy of the north have made use of their historical relationship with Islam to define themselves in ethnic/class terms and to justify their continued rule of the 'conquered' or 'subject' peoples (as the Gonja refer to the various other ethnic groups from the lower class). Indeed, a number of these people have turned to evangelical Christianity as a revolutionary force that will liberate them from what they see as their Muslim overlords (Ray *et al*., 1984). (This example is not intended to imply anything negative about Islam or

Christianity, but merely to illustrate how religion can be used in politics.)

Ethnically, Ghana is a very diverse country. Some one hundred ethnic groups contribute to Ghana's richness of cultural heritage, as well as to considerable political tensions in both historical and contemporary times.

If the officers of the British Empire had looked south when they established what became Ghana's northern boundary in 1898, they would have seen a good number of pre-colonial indigenous states that had depended, as so many states do today, on ethnicity to provide part of the ideological cohesion of their power structure. These political entities had included, among others, the Gonja, Dagomba, Mamprusi and Nanumba kingdoms of the north and the expanding Asante Confederacy, the smaller kingdoms, confederations and city states of the Ewe, the Fante, the Ga and the Nzima of the south.

The imposition of British imperial rule fossilized pre-colonial political and ethnic relationships. Given another century without European competition, perhaps the Asante Confederacy would have conquered and assimilated all the remaining independent political units in what are now Ghana, Ivory Coast, Burkina Faso and Togo. Perhaps some other kingdom would have played 'England' in a West African 'Britain'. However, the process of forcible nation-state building, so typical of Europe and North America, was put to an end to by British rule and the foundation for ethnic mistrust was laid. Once the British had broken the pre-colonial states' own monopolies of violence, they were quite ready to manipulate ethnic tensions through their policy of divide and rule. The British introduced elements of indirect rule, even to the extent of allowing, aiding and recognizing the re-introduction of the Asante Confederacy in 1935.

Two major results have flowed from this policy which are relevant to today's politics in Ghana. First, the aristocracies of Ghana have had a certain recognition and legitimation for their power over people and land entrenched in the constitutions of independent Ghana (Arhin, forthcoming; Ninsin, forthcoming). There has thus been a dual sovereignty implicit not only in the constitutions but also in the thinking of many in Ghana.

This leads us to the second result. There has been a lack of political integration as people debate whether to act as members of the new state or as members of an ethnic group that has roots which predate the new state. Are they Ghanaian or are they Asante, Ewe, Ga, Fante, Gonja, Dagomba, etc.? Will they or will they not be at a disadvantage if they do not invoke clan and ethnic ties with others of the same group? Thus, governments have come to be interpreted by many Ghanaians according to their ethnic affiliations. The accusation of 'tribalism', i.e. favouring those from one region or ethnic group, is hurled at political opponents to damage them, whether or not the accusations are justified.[1] Ethnicity has been an important political consideration that has cut across party lines and stunted the growth of class consciousness among workers, peasants and even the owners of plantations, factories, trading enterprises and other businesses.

The reality of misnamed 'tribal wars' is a complex mixture of class[2] and ethnic tensions which has its roots in the economy and in the structure of society. For example, in the north the wars between the Gonja and the Vagala (1980), the Nanumba and the Konkomba (1981) and the Mamprusi and the Kusasi (1984) have all been violent struggles between ethnic groups/classes in which the first-named were the aristocracy, and the latter the commoners. At stake was access to land, labour and tribute. The commoners beat the nobles in the last two of these.

Similarly, economics have been at the root of two other ethnic problems. The Busia regime's expulsion from Ghana of thousands of West African migrant workers in November 1969 has been regarded as an attempt to divert the attention of Ghanaians away from their economic problems (Chazan, 1983). Lebanese and Syrian traders were regarded with hostility in some quarters, more because of their wealth than because of their ethnic difference from the majority of the population. One of the senior economic advisers to the Chairman of the PNDC was in fact a Ghanaian of Lebanese origin. Racism is not a problem in Ghana and foreigners are almost universally treated with great friendliness and tolerance.

The ethnic and religious diversity has given a richness to Ghana's material culture. Asante can be likened to the 'kingdom of gold' because of its gold jewellery and the gleaming bronze weights used in the gold trade. The wooden stools made in the south are comfortable and aesthetically pleasing. The cloth of Ghana is richly coloured, ranging from patches and patterns of reds, golds, oranges and yellows in the south, to the legendary indigo blues from the Daboya pits in the north. The cuisine can be exquisite: *dagbli* is made from water yams, 'garden egg' vegetable is a bitter-sweet small white squash, and the taste of the 'grasscutter's' meat resembles that of dark turkey meat. Stews are made with meat and fish; pepper soups put vindaloos to shame. The range of architectural styles is intriguing: white-washed, mud-walled mosques that bristle like porcupines with their protruding wood supports, coastal castles, Project 600—a contemporary multistorey office block and official residence on the State House grounds in Accra—and Kumasi 'family' houses.

Historical Setting of the Revolution

Ghana's previous millenniums were marked by the migrations of hunting and fishing peoples, their settlement of the land, their development of agriculture and metal technologies as well as long-distance trade, and the growth of village and urban life.[3] All of this laid the economic and social basis for the rise of distinct states during the eleventh to the mid-fifteenth centuries (Anquandah, 1982b). The growth of gold-mining drew three Akan states in what is now central Ghana into long-distance, international trade. At first the trade focused to the north on the ancient Mali Kingdom, across the Sahara to North Africa's ports, and finally to European and Asian markets. After 1470, the first direct contact with European traders—Portuguese in this case—the gold trade with Europe increasingly by-passed North Africa. Instead, the gold was directed southwards to the Atlantic coast, along which were built castles, forts and trading posts by the Portuguese, Dutch, Danes, British, Germans and French (Wilks, 1976).

The gold and slave trades enhanced the financial and military capabilities of the various pre-colonial Ghanaian states. Increasingly, this gave them access to firearms and gunpowder which were instrumental in altering the balances of power between the indigenous states. In Ghana, as in Europe, the sixteenth, seventeenth and eighteenth centuries were the period of the birth, growth, destruction and consolidation of states (Boahen, 1966).

Before turning to what emerged as the proto-Ghanaian state, Asante,[4] it is important to note that to the east of Accra, along the mouth and southern stretches of the Volta, the Ewe (who were not Akan) formed some one hundred and twenty mini-states (Greene, 1981), and that to the west of the Ga of Accra were more than twenty Fante mini-republics, as well as Nzima. All of these came under the influence and control of the Asante empire. The Fante developed close ties with British merchants from the 1600s onwards. They benefited greatly from this association, acting as middlemen in the slave trade. Ultimately, their disputes with the Asante empire led to the colonization of both by the British by the late 1800s.

Asante arose as a principality in the Denkyira kingdom. Denkyira lay to the north of the Fante and in the western part of what is now Ghana, but to the south of Asante which came to be centred in Kumasi. After a period of initial consolidation, King (or Asantehene) Osei Tutu defeated the Denkyira state in 1701. The Asante empire then began to expand rapidly in all directions. Osei Tutu was succeeded by Opuku Ware, whose thirty-year rule combined the military qualities of Prussia's Frederick the Great with the administrative and economic abilities of Russia's Peter the Great. By 1824, the Asante empire stretched north to exercise varying degrees of control over the Gonja, Dagomba and Nanumba kingdoms in what is now the Northern Region of Ghana, east into what is now Togo, west into what is now Ivory Coast, and south to the coast, apart from the European forts. By the early 1800s, Asante controlled over 100,000 sq. mls. and some two to three million people (Wilks, 1976). However, despite the Asante victory over a British-led army in 1824, they were ultimately defeated in 1874, 1896 and 1900 by other British armies backed by the industrial might of this even greater empire (Arhin, 1967; Boahen, 1974; Fynn, 1971, 1982a).

The first stage in the fossilization of these pre-colonial states came in January 1471 when two Portuguese ships reached the Ghanaian coast in search of trade, exploration being merely one of the necessary preliminaries. Eleven years later, the Portuguese traders established the first European fort in Ghana at Elmina, using first persuasion and then hints of force to gain the consent of the local king. This firmly established the pattern of relationships between Europeans and

Africans in the area that has since been modified by variations in the balance of power. The question has been how equal a partnership there was to be.

European powers scrambled to control the trade with what is now Ghana. So much gold was exported that the coast became known as the Gold Coast. Besides gold, other exported goods included ivory, timber, animal skins, rice and slaves. European goods imported into Ghana included manufactured goods such as schnapps and brandies, other consumer goods such as clothing and cutlery, and weaponry—especially firearms. Some might question whether the pattern of trade has really changed much in over five centuries: primary products out, manufactured goods in.

The British conquest of Asante allowed them to formalize their control over the south as the Gold Coast Colony and to penetrate past the Asante barrier. By 1898, most of the north was part of the British empire, the French and Germans having agreed on common boundaries with the British in this part of Africa. The 1901 British Order in Council created three colonies with slightly differing statuses: the Colony, the coast and inland area south of Asante, became a colony by settlement. Ashanti (or Asante) became a colony by conquest. The Northern Territories became a protectorate. In 1914, Britain quickly added parts of former German Togo to what became Ghana. In 1934, Britain united the three colonies into the Gold Coast. Britain thus created the present legal boundaries of Ghana and laid the administrative basis for the future state.

British interests had been both strategic and commercial in expanding their control inland. Both gold and slave trades could be carried out from coastal enclaves. The export of slaves supplanted the export of gold. However, in 1807 Britain abolished the slave trade. New economic opportunities for British business in colonial Ghana became apparent in a variety of tropical agricultural products and new gold-mining techniques. By 1914, large amounts of cocoa, palm oil (used in soap), timber, rubber and gold were being exported. Railways were built into the interior to facilitate this trade.

As Ghana was drawn further into the global market, three groups benefited particularly from the restructured economic activity. British firms which were able to control the import–export trade and credit made enormous profits. Those Ghanaians who had control over land—usually the nobility or chiefs—were able to employ migrant labourers and share-croppers to grow the cocoa. All of these benefited, those with land rights benefiting the most in many cases. The British colonial authorities benefited from the taxes levied on the various enterprises. These taxes paid for the salaries and benefits of the colonial officials, the military occupation, as well as for limited transportation, communication and social service facilities.

The contribution made by the British occupation of Ghana should not be underestimated. The costs should not be ignored either, however. At a time when government in Britain was becoming increasingly democratic, British rule in Ghana did not extend the same rights to Ghanaians until the 1950s, shortly before independence. British rule was authoritarian and lacked the consent of the Ghanaians as expressed by that formula of legitimacy 'one person, one vote'. The British governed and traded for their own benefit, the aspirations of Ghanaians were of secondary importance. After 1945 large sums of foreign exchange belonging to the cocoa farmers were 'borrowed' by the British government to bolster the British currency rather than being left with the Ghanaians to invest and spend as they saw fit (Fitch & Oppenheimer, 1966). Hence, investment priorities became distorted. The eventual integration of Ghana and Ghanaians into the world market was a very uneven one. The railway was not extended into the north because the British could not find a crop worth exporting from there. The north thus remained poorer in terms of income and services such as schools and medical facilities. (These problems were later addressed more fully by Nkrumah's nationalist governments.) Even in those areas most fully penetrated by capitalism, great disparities in income remained. Nevertheless, there was a postwar cocoa boom under British rule and some of the fruits of this boom produced by the Ghanaians were spent by the British on social services. At independence, after six years of joint rule by Britain and Nkrumah, one in four Ghanaians was literate in the official language, English. This compares very favourably with the neglect of African education by the Portuguese in their three African colonies over a similar period of time. Segal estimated that 99 per cent of the Africans were illiterate and that less than 4 per cent could speak Portuguese (Segal, 1962).

The nationalist movement grew up within this context. Ghanaian nationalism was also influenced by the decline of the British Empire and the growing power of the Soviet Union. Britain's economic and military power were sapped during the Second World War: parts of the British Empire fell to the Nazis and to the Japanese. Ghanaian troops fought in defence of the Empire and saw how the British were not all-powerful. The possibility of challenging the British Empire became more of a reality, especially given the concessions that the British government had been making. Indeed, in British liberal and socialist circles, there was a movement to support decolonization on both ethical and political grounds. These ideas were influential not only within the ruling post-war Labour government but also among a growing number of Ghanaian nationalists in direct or indirect contact with the left of Britain and other countries.

The most significant of these other countries for left nationalists in the immediate post-war era was of course the Soviet Union. There were a number of reasons for this. The Soviet Union was seen as having been victorious over the Nazis who had defeated colonial powers such as France and Belgium that had African territories, and who had come close to defeating the British Empire. The military and economic might of the first socialist state was impressive. Not only was the Soviet Union one of the powerful victorious allies, but its leaders argued against colonial domination and were in favour of the independence of the colonized peoples. Moreover, this power had been accomplished by the state in its search for socialism. The Soviet Union was also willing to put modest resources at the disposal of those whom it perceived to be progressive and this included some Ghanaian nationalists. This is not to argue that Ghanaian nationalism was the creation of the Soviet Union: the birth in 1897 of an early nationalist organization, the Aborigines' Rights Protection Society, before the 1917 Soviet revolution, should confirm that. In addition, the society was founded by typical upper-class nationalists—professionals, such as lawyers and others. By 1949 Ghanaian nationalism contained a wide variety of political opinion, ranging from conservative elitist lawyers to socialists.

In 1946, British concessions to African demands for representation had resulted in an elected majority of Africans in the Legislative Council in Ghana. The British Governor still controlled the executive, however, so it was not responsible government. Moreover, Ghana remained a British colony. In 1947, J. B. Danquah created the United Gold Coast Convention (UGCC) which sought self-government alone. The UGCC membership was mainly composed of a Western-educated elite: lawyers, businessmen, doctors and senior civil servants. As part of the UGCC's campaign to broaden its appeal to other sectors, the UGCC brought Kwame Nkrumah back to Ghana in 1947. Nkrumah quickly rose to political prominence after his unjustified arrest by the British during the 1948 economic riots in which ex-servicemen were shot while demanding better pensions, together with an end to inflation and unemployment. There was also resentment against the British government for using the Cocoa Marketing Board to skim off much of the profit from African cocoa farmers. When the UGCC conservatives began to dissociate themselves from Nkrumah, the latter formed the Convention People's Party (CPP) which replaced the UGCC. Also as a result of the riots, in 1950 the British announced a new constitution which added an executive partially responsible to the legislature.

In the subsequent February 1951 general elections, Nkrumah's CPP conveniently won a majority of seats in the legislature. The British then released him from prison and appointed him *de facto* Prime Minister. In 1952 Nkrumah became the first African Prime Minister in the Commonwealth. During the first phase of Nkrumah's rule (1951-7), effective power was divided between the British government and Nkrumah's CPP government. As the constitutions mutated and Nkrumah won each of the successive elections in 1954 and 1956, the British government recognized Ghanaian independence under Nkrumah's CPP to be inevitable. In response, Britain gradually (and somewhat reluctantly) transferred more powers to the legislative assembly, elected by universal suffrage in 1954. On 3 August 1956, this Assembly passed a unanimous motion calling for independence.

Ghana became independent on 6 March 1957, the 113th anniversary of the signing of the Fante Bond between the British and the Fante which had led to the expansion of British administration throughout Ghana. The new Ghanaian government was a unitary, unicameral parliament with an executive responsible to parliament which was elected on the basis of one person, one vote. Ghana became a republic on 1 July 1960, following Nkrumah's victory in the republican plebiscite. In the wake of the one-party state's creation in 1964, Nkrumah's CPP, not unexpectedly, won the 1965 general elections. However, while Nkrumah was absent abroad, a group of right-wing military officers overthrew his government in a coup that began on 23 February 1966 and succeeded the next day. Lieutenant-General Joseph Ankrah was appointed Chairman of the National Liberation Council (NLC). The NLC lasted until 1969.

The accomplishments of Nkrumah and his movement were considerable.[5] Nkrumah led Ghana to independence. He created the political symbols and political psychology of patriotism and sovereignty in Ghana against which all others are still measured, and which to the left are still the touchstone of truth. Nearly twenty years after his overthrow, the front pages of Ghanaian newspapers, under the PNDC, contain quotes from his speeches and writings.

Nkrumah's government rapidly expanded educational and health services across the country. Hospitals and clinics, schools and universities became part of his legacy to Ghana. He built Tema into an industrial city, one of Ghana's two man-made ocean-going ports. He brought many import-substitution industries to Ghana, thus expanding the urban working class. The Volta dam was constructed, providing the electricity needed to power the aluminium refineries and other industries and cities in the south as well as neighbouring countries (though not the north). His state enterprises ranged from shipping, to an airline, to agriculture. He had started to create the economic infrastructure that Ghana needed if it were to become an efficient exporter of primary goods, let alone to break free from its dependent position on the resource periphery.

However, while such a strategy of state involvement in the economy can result in the building of the economic preconditions for socialism, it can, and has been, used to perform work at public expense for private entrepreneurs—as in the case of areas ranging from industrial Britain to resource-exporting Canada (Nelles, 1974; Pratt, 1977). Moreover, such strategies are expensive. Vast amounts of foreign exchange were spent on building this infrastructure and productive capacity. Mismanagement and corruption did occur and some resources were wasted.

Economic problems grew as production failed to keep pace with expenditure.

Nkrumah's downfall was caused by a combination of internal and external factors. As economic problems grew, Nkrumah turned to the Western capitalist countries for foreign investment and loans. Yet at the same time he attempted to improve Ghana's relations with the Soviet Union—behaviour not guaranteed to win the hearts of the Western cold war contenders. Educational agreements with Eastern European countries sent Ghanaian students to those countries. Officers of Nkrumah's Presidential regiment were trained in the Soviet Union: this marked a departure from the old colonial pattern of using overseas training centres in Britain. (Other countries which supplied training after independence included Canada and Israel, which was later replaced by India.) Some army officers believed this threatened the social unity of the officer corps. The American CIA saw Nkrumah as leading Ghana into Soviet domination. The CIA was behind the right-wing Ghanaian officers who staged the coup and led the NLC (1966–69).

The power of Nkrumah's regime to resist the coup had been seriously weakened by several factors. Growing economic problems had led to the disaffection of groups which had formerly been supporters of Nkrumah. For example, the stringent suppression of the 1961 workers' strikes by the government led to the erosion of working-class support for Nkrumah. Moreover, despite his declared intention to build scientific socialism in Ghana, he did not consolidate a socialist base, in particular by constructing a socialist vanguard party. Part of Nkrumah's problem was in trying to build a Marxist–Leninist party when he was not yet sufficiently determined or knowledgeable to do so. Furthermore, Nkrumah's existing party, the CPP, contained very few people with an effective grasp of Marxism–Leninism. In the 1950s the CPP had been a broadly-based party. Consequently, there was a large faction among the leadership who, while agreed on the need for independence, sought to promote their own economic interests by nurturing the full flower of capitalism: they did not want socialism. They constituted the largest part of the CPP leadership (Card, 1975; Reeck, 1976).

Nkrumah had a certain leeway (Folson, 1977): he was able to

establish an ideological training institute at Winneba. But few who attended understood what they taught or were taught. A few did, however, and Nkrumah was able to gather around him a number of foreign and domestic socialists of nearly all types. They had some effect in trying to establish the economic preconditions of socialism by promoting state control of the economy (the state is still the largest employer in Ghana), and by establishing a youth movement, the Young Pioneers, which transmitted socialist values to some of its youthful members. Some of these young people went on to become senior figures in the December 31st Revolution (interview with Captain Kojo Tsikata, Accra, 1 August 1984). Despite the failure to create a socialist party, Nkrumah did help to broaden the contact of Ghanaians with socialism. His nationalism was the intellectual and emotional launching pad for many Ghanaian socialists. Some Ghanaians, impressed by what Nkrumah tried to do with Ghana's economy, were inspired to imagine what socialism might do for their country. Nkrumah shaped the coming generation of socialists who were to seize power on 31 December 1981.

The military government, which called itself the National Liberation Council,[6] ruled from 24 February 1966 to September 1969. During this time they conducted a campaign against what they considered to be manifestations of socialism. The military junta banned the CPP, harassed former CPP leaders and issued decrees preventing many of them from running for elected offices in the future. The junta privatized a number of state enterprises, denounced socialism and broke off diplomatic relations with Eastern bloc countries. However, the junta were unable to solve Ghana's political and economic problems by their 'return' to private enterprise. In response to IMF urging, not only were state corporations sold off, but the currency was devalued. Unemployment grew and the poorer people found the price of imported goods growing beyond their reach. This was a period of disorganization for the left in Ghana.

The Second Republic (September 1969 to January 1972) was led by the elected civilian government of Prime Minister Kofi Busia's Progress Party.[7] Despite a certain democratic promise at the start of Busia's conservative government, Busia quickly became authoritarian and unable to deal with the growing economic problems. In 1971 he banned the Trade Union Congress (TUC) in response to major strikes. Cocoa prices dropped in 1971, sparking off an economic crisis reminiscent of Nkrumah's last days in power. Busia devalued the Cedi by 45 per cent in 1971: on 13 January 1972, the Second Republic was overthrown by another military junta.

From 13 January 1972 to 4 June 1979, a series of corrupt generals ruled Ghana through military juntas, variously entitled the National Redemption Council (1972–5), led by General I. Acheampong; the Supreme Military Council (1975–5 July 1978), led again by Acheampong; and the Supreme Military Council II (5 July 1978–4 June 1979). Despite some early rhetorical phrases about socialism and anti-imperialism, these governments were marked by a devotion to personal greed.[8] The corruption, the economic crisis and the anti-democratic beliefs of these juntas were, as later chapters argue, key elements in the rise of a new generation of socialists who were brought to power initially as 'Robin Hood' nationalists during the Armed Forces Revolutionary Council (AFRC) of the June 4th 1979 uprisings. Although they handed over power to President Hilla Limann's Third republic,[9] their taste of power, Limann's ineffectiveness in solving Ghana's economic crisis and in dealing with them led to Limann's fall on 31 December 1981.

2   The Formation of the December 31st Revolution

Political forces led by Flight-Lieutenant Jerry John Rawlings have twice assumed power in Ghana: once on 4th June 1979 and again on 31st December 1981. There has been considerable debate within the December 31st forces over the revolutionary strategies and tactics needed to achieve a populist and socialist society.

The rise of this Marxist-led revolutionary movement must be seen in the context of several factors. First, Ghanaian Marxists have been profoundly affected by their perceptions of Kwame Nkrumah's successful drive for Ghanaian independence from Britain (1949–57), his attempts to move towards scientific socialism in his independence governments (1957–66), and his writings on this following his overthrow in 1966. Second, there has been a tradition among these elements of critically analysing the Ghanaian state, economy and society as it floundered under governments perceived to be ineffective and/or corrupt, as well as fundamentally unconcerned with the fate of Ghanaians (excepting the rulers' families and friends). Third, there has been much debate over what role they should play in relation to the Ghanaian state (i.e., change by joining it, change by criticism from the sidelines, or change by overthrow). Fourth, they have debated how to build socialism in Ghana after the overthrow of the Western/bourgeois-orientated government of President Hilla Limann, the same administration to which Rawlings had handed over control on 24 September 1979.

Key elements in the December 31 Revolution, having seized state power, refocused their efforts on organizational initiatives. Significant revolution-building strategies which included the creation of anti-corruption tribunals, People's Defence Committees (PDCs), Workers' Defence Committees and People's Shops. These must be seen in the context of the need to build a central revolutionary political party, to protect the revolution from overthrow, to gain control over Ghana's public administration (and to revitalize it), and to deal with those perceived as having caused Ghana's economic near-collapse.

How the Revolution Started: The First Hours

The revolution was initiated as an insurrection without the existence, let alone the backing, of an organized, coherently-articulated revolutionary party. At 3.00 a.m. on 31 December 1981, Flight-Lieutenant Jerry John Rawlings led a small band of between eight and forty (accounts differ) Ghana armed forces junior ranks and armed civilians against the civilian government of President Hilla Limann. At midnight, after yet another round of parties by the Limann regime, the revolutionaries held the element of surprise: they began to round up President and parliament amid the debris of the old regime (interviews, Accra, July–August 1984). Vice-President de Graft-Johnson's surrender on 6 January 1982 (*Ghanaian Times*, 7 January 1982) was a signal for the irreversible collapse of the Third Republic. The armed forces and the police were reluctant to defend the Limann Republic. Key positions in Accra were seized, including the headquarters and radio facilities of the Ghana Broadcasting Corporation (GBC). Rawlings' early morning broadcast rallied support. He declared, 'Fellow citizens of Ghana, as you would have noticed we are not playing the National Anthem. In other words this is not a coup. I ask for nothing less than a revolution. Something that would transform the social and economic order of this country.'

This then was the central problem faced by Rawlings and his allies: how to turn an insurrection into a revolution. However, we must first examine the causes behind the events of December 1981 in order to evaluate the various revolutionary strategies.

The Roots of the Revolution

In his 31 December speech Rawlings outlined (Rawlings, 31 December 1981) a number of his revolutionary goals—providing an insight into the causes of the revolution. The first and most important was one made in his first paragraph, namely that he believed Ghana's economy and society to have become subject to such distorting forces that much more than a military coup was needed: only a revolution would succeed in reviving Ghana.

The leaders of the previous regime were characterized as dominated by 'a pack of criminals'. Their domination had been made possible because the military (especially the junior ranks), and ordinary Ghanaians generally had been excluded from the real decision-making processes. What was needed, therefore, was not merely military rule but a fundamental restructuring of the relations between production, distribution and power. The previous Ghanaian generals amply refuted the idea of the military *per se* as inherent 'modernizers' or developers. (See Huntington 1968 and Janowitz 1964 for discussions of this idea which was popularized in certain circles in the 1960s.) Rawlings maintained that only a revolution would incorporate into decision-making 'the masses . . . the people, the farmers, the police, the soldiers, the workers'. Interestingly enough, he also included 'the rich', but this was qualified by the general context which suggested that these would be the patriotic, democratic and uncorrupted elements of the rich, not the 'criminals' in the PNP hierarchy. (This was reminiscent of Mao's 'new democracy' strategy.[1] a theme which was to be developed more fully in later days.) Rawlings' notion of the necessity for revolution thus included the desire for a cleansing of society and its reintegration where possible. Again, like Mao, Rawlings saw the need for Ghanaians to defend their country's economy against hostile external forces (Mao, 1939 and 1940). This anti-imperialist thrust was combined with the pan-Africanism of Kwame Nkrumah.[2] Rawlings argued that the Ghanaian achievement of 'social and economic democracy' under the revolution would encourage other African states and would lead to the emergence of a strong, unified, continental state that would be capable of competing even with the United States.

A second set of reasons were more personal. Rawlings characterized the harassment by the Limann government of certain former AFRC leaders, including himself, and other revolutionary leaders, as 'a whole lot of callous things some of us have gone through'. This was then generalized by Rawlings to the whole population, as their having experienced 'two years of nothing but repression' under PNP rule. As will shortly be seen, the attacks by the Limann government, and their military intelligence in particular, on Rawlings and his friends played a signficant part in precipitating the latters' action.

The speech contained much less about action than an attempt at legitimation. The first directive issued as a result of Rawlings' speech was the reinstatement of the Army Commander and the Chief of Defence Staff from the 1979 ARFC period, Rawlings' first insurrection. Rawlings denied that the soldiers were going to shoot all their officers. He warned outside powers against trying to mount an invasion. He briefly mentioned the existence of a new, though as yet unnamed ruling council, and the decision to establish a 'People's Defence Organization next to a National Defence Organization', but no functions were outlined for these bodies.

The action content of the speech revealed a concern to facilitate the goals of the revolution by attempting to contribute to the establishment of the new regime. The speech indicated two sets of causes of the revolution: continuing crisis in the economy, society and politics of Ghana and a set of trigger factors that focused on individual revolutionary leaders, most notably Rawlings and Captain Kojo Tsikata.

The long-term crisis factors and the response to them by the revolutionaries clearly place the December 31st revolution in what Szajkowski has termed the third period of the establishment of Marxist regimes which are 'intrinsically linked with resurgent Caribbean, Cuban, African, Arab and Asian nationalism in general and the successful conclusion of several long-drawn-out national liberation struggles in particular' (Szajkowski, 1982, p. 168). The perceived need for national rebirth became married to Marxism as a response to what was perceived as the only solution to a long period of national 'decay' in Ghana.

The December 31st revolutionary leadership saw the roots of Ghana's problems as having been particularly revealed during General I. K. Acheampong's rule (13 January 1972 to 5 July 1978) and to a lesser but still significant extent during that of General F. W. K. Akuffo's following eleven-month rule up to his overthrow on 4 June 1979 by Rawlings (interviews in Accra with PNDC members, J. J. Rawlings, 7 August 1984 and Justice D. F. Annan, 4 August 1984). Others have noted the growing depth of the economic crisis during this time (e.g. Jeffries, July 1982; Kraus, March–April 1982 and March 1983; and Oquaye, 1980). Part of the crisis has been seen as 'the economic consequences of the military regimes during 1972–1979' (Kraus, March 1983, p. 116).

The crisis was signalled for this period by a number of factors: negative economic growth, balance of payments deficits for most years, an average yearly 3 per cent decline in the per capita Gross Domestic Product, inflation averaged at 46.6 per cent per year, cocoa farmers' revenues decreased from an index of 100 in 1963 to 78 in 1972, and 49 in 1979 (Kraus, March 1983, p. 116). As Oquaye (1980, p. 28) shows, citing National Consumer Price Index figures, inflation was at a moderate level in the civilian government period preceding military rule, but rapidly took off during the time of the generals: 1970–1, 4.8 per cent; 1971–2, 11.8 per cent; 1972–3, 8.6 per cent; but 1973–4, 23.4 per cent. The figures for inflation were: 1976, 53 per cent; 1977, 116 per cent; for 1978, 74 per cent; for 1979, 54 per cent (Kraus, March 1983, p. 116). Towards the end of Limann's rule, inflation was roaring like a bush fire, at 121 per cent (Kraus, March–April 1982, p. 64; figures for 1 July 1980 to 31 July 1981).

The Limann government's failure to solve the economic crisis, and the political corruption that it engendered, contributed significantly to its overthrow (Chazan, 1983, pp. 311–2; Kraus, March–April 1982, pp. 59, 62, 64–6; Kraus, March 1983, pp. 115 and 117). How much of the economic crisis was actually due to the Limann government is open to question (Kraus, March–April 1982, pp. 65–6; interview with the Chairman of the PNDC, Flight-Lieutenant J. J. Rawlings, Accra, 7 August 1984). Several factors which contributed to the crisis appear to have been not of Limann's making. As the inflation figures above illustrate, the economic crisis had been increasing in scope and intensity for quite some time. Limann inherited a chaos of policy created by previous regimes, most notably that of General Acheampong. Both the external and internal economic situations had been deteriorating: the combination of administrative mismanagement and the declining price of cocoa meant that by 1981 farmers were receiving in real value only 14 per cent of the 1963 price (Kraus, March–April, 1982, p. 65).

Limann could still have taken action on a number of economic issues. He could have increased prices for cocoa production and hence the potential for foreign exchange earnings. He, should not, perhaps, have promised to greatly increase the supply of consumer goods when the foreign exchange reserves were inadequate. He should not have allowed the Members of Parliament to grant themselves salaries grossly disproportionate to what the average Ghanaian earned, which created an economic grievance against the government. Limann also appointed a number of ministers and state corporation officials who were perceived to be inept.

Limann did not face the problem issues of devaluation and price controls. The official Cedi was over-valued at US $1.00 = 2.75, when the real but illegal price was US $1.00 = 25 in 1980 and 42 at the end of Limann's regime (Kraus, March–April 1982, pp. 65–6). It has been argued that devaluation was necessary for Ghana's economic recovery (Jeffries, July 1982, pp. 308, 312, 315–16; Kraus, March–April 1982, p. 66). By not devaluing the Cedi, Limann was unable to take advantage of a potential increase in Ghana's ability to export goods as their prices became more competitive or, more importantly, to 'increase the effective price to local producers [thus], providing incentives for reinvestment and production', in this way decisively shifting profitability from trader to producer. Related to this question was the ineffective application of price controls. Instead of working to provide a 'fair' return for the producer and an affordable item for the poor and middle-income classes, enormous sums were transferred to traders by corrupt practices (Kraus, March–April, 1982, p. 66), for two main reasons. First, the state structures had lost much of their capacity to enforce policy (Chazan, 1983). Second, significant numbers of those who ruled and those who administered had become tainted by a context of corruption.

Corruption has characterized the sick, soft underbelly of successive governments in Ghana, a festering sore in the Ghanaian body politic that gradually spreads its poison, *inter alia*, aborting one embryonic regime after another. Certainly this has been true of the soldiery, who have conducted coups from 1966 onwards (Kirk-Greene, 1981; Okeke, 1982; Chazan, 1983). Corruption is of course not a uniquely African phenomenon: the histories of Canada, the United States and Britain are full of examples of corruption.

The corruption or '*kalabule*' of the Acheampong period (1972–8) has stood out as a pinnacle of decadence which ranged from overcharging for goods and services to 'a system whereby top officials issued chits [giving loans or import licences] to young women who paraded the corridors of power offering themselves for libidinal pleasure in return for favours' (Oquaye, 1980, p. 17, cf. pp. 20–1, 40 *re* sex, and *passim*, pp. 17–55. See also Jeffries, 1982, p. 314). Of course, corruption was not necessarily the major cause of Ghana's economic and political crisis,[3] but it was the catalyst for the Rawlings-inspired insurrection of 4 June 1979, which in turn was the forerunner of the December 31 1981 revolution (Okeke, 1982; Hansen & Collins, January 1980; Oquaye, 1980, pp. 133–5).

By the end of General Acheampong's rule there was a sense in some quarters, not least the junior ranks—which included Rawlings—that the senior officers of the armed forces and police and their civilian counterparts were no longer fit to rule. These young people saw a general picture of decadence and greed that had ramifications far beyond the self-satisfaction of any one corrupt official, businessman or businesswoman. First, the image of a 'pure' military in the minds of Ghanaian civilians had been tainted by the example of the Acheampong regime. This stain had not been erased by the gentle 'retirement' of Acheampong by General Akuffo in July 1978. There is much to be said for the argument that the June 4th 1979 insurrection was an attempt by the junior ranks to restore the honour of the Ghanaian military by eliminating the symbols of military decadence (generals, including three former military heads of state—Afrifa, Acheampong and Akuffo—were shot for corruption and numerous officers, officials and business people were also jailed for corruption). Having 'cleansed' the armed forces, the junior ranks could retire to their barracks with honour (Hansen & Collins, 1980).

Second, the diversion of increasingly scarce resources away from their 'proper' or optimum use for the public good meant that the economic and political infrastructure of the country was stagnating and decaying. Statistics became increasingly unreliable through the 1970s: the last report of the Ministry of Agriculture was issued in 1979 (interview, Librarian, Ministry of Agriculture Library, Accra, 14 June 1983). As the corrupt officers and civilians wasted Ghana's foreign exchange reserves, imported goods such as medicines, spare parts and raw materials for factories, were no longer available when needed. The consequences of the corruption in aggravating Ghana's economic crisis were well known among Ghanaians. The power and prestige of the senior officers were broken by the junior ranks during the AFRC days of 1979 in response to these perceptions (interview, PNDC member, Justice D. F. Annan, Accra, 4 August 1984). Under the impression that the AFRC had succeeded in refurbishing the country, and for other reasons too, Rawlings and the rest of the AFRC handed over the reins of government to the new civilian government of President Hilla Limann. But Limann was unable to reaffirm the effective authority of the colonels and generals over the junior ranks, to solve the economic crisis or prevent the re-emergence of corruption.

Rawlings has stated that he initiated the December 31st revolution partly because, as he perceived, the Limann government was, like its predecessor, riddled with corruption:

Since the government was still perceived by the people as a remote, alien institution [imposed by colonialism], they watched helplessly as successive regimes raped the country, until graft and corruption permeated every level of society, whilst the economy reached the point of disintegration [interview, Accra, 7 August 1984].

This statement is consistent with his speech of 31 December 1981.

Reasons of a more personal kind also played a part in Rawlings' decision to initiate the revolution at the time he did. His presence in Ghana, his constant criticism of the Limann government and his association with the two major Marxist organizations (the June 4th Movement and the New Democratic Movement) combined to threaten President Limann with a potential coup every day of his presidential term. During 1981, the Limann regime made public its fears, real or perceived, that Rawlings and a number of his associates were planning a coup. Consequently, Military Intelligence mounted one of its more heavy-handed and clumsy surveillance and harassment operations of the leadership of the revolutionary movements.

Military Intelligence took Rawlings for what was supposed to have been a one-way midnight car ride that should have been reminiscent of American gangster movies but, ended up as the Keystone Cops! A sympathetic junior officer in Military Intelligence warned Rawlings that, when the car stopped in the hills outside Accra, Rawlings should not attempt to escape. Later, when the car came to a stop, Rawlings looked out of the suspiciously-unlocked door and saw that an armoured car had its machine gun trained on his 'escape-route': he would have been the victim of the classic 'shot-while-escaping' story. Instead of 'escaping' Rawlings stayed where he was and was shortly released. On another occasion, one of the other leaders, Captain Kojo Tsikata, was injured when his car was crashed off the road by Military Intelligence. Rawlings rushed to his rescue and his presence saved the Captain from further fatal harm.

The Limann government had clearly signalled its intentions to the potential revolutionaries. Rawlings and some of the other top leaders, therefore, faced a limited range of futures: death or exile. Rawlings stunned Limann and his administration by choosing a third alternative: revolution. Metaphorically speaking, Limann reached for his gun first, but Rawlings was the better shot. Fear for their own safety, therefore, played a significant role in the revolutionaries' decision to initiate the revolution itself.

3 The Development of the Revolutionary Strategy

The revolutionary strategy that has emerged in Ghana since 31 December 1981 reflects the precipitous inauguration of the revolution, its consequent reliance on Rawlings' charisma as a temporary substitute for the expected revolutionary party, splits within the PNDC, and Mao's strategy of 'New Democracy'.

Rawlings' inaugural speech, as suggested in the previous chapter, was much more sharply focused on the rationale of the insurrection than on providing a blueprint for the future. The speech as a whole has an urgency to it that, combined with its focus, suggests it was quickly drafted, though of course prudence does argue that potential revolutionaries ought not to travel about with their 'overthrow' speech in their pockets too far in advance of that event. The fact that the initial composition of the new supreme governing body, the Provisional National Defence Council (PNDC) was not announced until twelve days after the revolution again suggests the hasty nature of the revolution's inception. Also indicative is the fact that only the preamble to the PNDC's policy book has been published—and that not until five months after the beginning of the revolution (PNDC, Preamble, May, 1982).

The revolution was then, arranged hastily, there was no organized revolutionary party, and the revolution depended very much on Rawlings' personality, skills and ability to inspire loyalty in certain key units of the armed forces. Rawlings' centrality to the revolutionary process highlights the importance of personal reasons in determining the timing of the revolution. Rawlings' considerable political skills have been amply demonstrated by his ability to overthrow two governments. He successfully transformed the discontent felt by the junior ranks against their superiors that had grown during the Acheampong, Akuffo and Limann regimes into a loyalty to himself. He was able to do this most notably by his declaration to the trial judges that he took all responsibility for the failed 15 May 1979 coup attempt, that his men were only 'following orders' and should therefore not be punished. What strikes the foreign observer (and also the Ghanaian observer: see interview with Justice D. F. Annan, PNDC member, Accra, 4 August 1984) is how poor relations between officers and men must have been if Rawlings' repeated declarations of loyalty to his men at their trial, taken in conjunction with his denunciation of corruption, could provoke his successful rescue by junior ranks from execution by the generals and could mobilize the support necessary to turn the tables on them.

At the onset of the revolution, the left was fragmented into some eight small, young organizations, as well as one that was older and larger. The largest organization was the African Youth Command (AYC), which claimed a membership of many tens of thousands and was formed in 1974. The orientation of the AYC was Pan-African and to a much lesser degree Marxist. However, despite its size and the distribution of its branches, the AYC had not played the central role that it could have. In part this appears to have been because it was not associated with Rawlings. Instead, two other movements, both Marxist, have been most influential in directing the course of the revolution, and Rawlings was involved in both of them. The June Fourth Movement (JFM) was formed with Rawlings as its nominal chairman after the Rawlings-led AFRC handed over power to President Limann. The New Democratic Movement (NDM) was also formed at the same time. Neither organization was national in distribution or had extensive links with the working class or peasantry and both had only a small number of members, the JFM being the larger. Both movements provided many members for the top revolutionary positions after 31 December 1981.

Despite their agreement on the necessity for building a socialist Ghana, the revolutionary strategies of the two movements differed significantly on the questions of timing and allies. The JFM wanted to move quickly to build a Bolshevik-style revolutionary party, attack the rich, and break all ties with imperialism, namely the International Monetary Fund, the World Bank and the governments and multinational companies of North America, Western Europe and Japan. In short, the JFM leadership wanted to move quickly into socialism, once the revolution started. The NDM also desired the accomplishment of socialism but argued that it would only be possible after a considerable time had elapsed. During this time, it was necessary for Ghanaian socialists to analyse their own society and to take action based on that new understanding. This approach reflected Mao's attempts to adapt and not blindly adopt Marxist–Leninism to his own country (see for example *Selected Works*, Vol. I, 1965).

As the New Democratic Movement's name suggests, the NDM has been influenced by Mao's strategy of 'new democracy' as an intermediate stage on the way to a fuller form of socialism. During the period of this intermediate stage, efforts were to be concentrated on developing a better understanding of Ghana, building a revolutionary workers' and peasants' party, making alliances with other classes, groups and factions willing to fight imperialism and rebuild Ghana's shattered economy.

These strategies were born before the parent organizations were catapulted into the December 31st Revolution. At first glance, the different revolutionary organizations and individuals faced a number of apparently daunting tasks demanding simultaneous action. The seizure of state power had to be completed. Revolutionary control of the state had to be defended. The insurrection had to be turned into a socialist revolution. Revolutionary structures, such as a party, had to be built. The administrative machinery of the old state had to be kept going, reactivated and redirected until new programmes and structures could be devised and implemented. The economy had to be resurrected. At second glance, these tasks nearly proved in practice to be overwhelming.

Before dealing with these tasks, it is important to examine the overall results of the interplay of these two strategies. From 31 December 1981 to 23 November 1982, a period of less than a year, both strategies competed for the attention and approval of the leaders of the revolution (part of their problem was the lack of an organized group of followers such as ordinary members of a Marxist–Leninist party). On the one hand, confiscation of the luxurious houses and cars of the rich and allegedly corrupt began. Foreign assistance was solicited from Libya and the various 'socialist' bloc countries. Imperialism was denounced daily in the newspapers. The formation of a thoroughgoing Marxist–Leninist party was urged. On the other hand, the inability of the Eastern bloc countries to furnish the huge amounts of capital needed to resuscitate the economy and the shortage of revolutionaries with the necessary expertise in managing the various sectors of the economy suggested the (hotly disputed) need to seek loans from the IMF and World Bank and to make allies with 'patriotic' professionals and business people as a prelude to a more conventional socialist economy.

Disagreements grew between the proponents of the two approaches during 1982, until senior elements of the JFM held a press conference at the end of October at which they announced that they had replaced Rawlings because they argued he was no longer revolutionary. Rawlings quickly announced that he was still Chairman of the PNDC, and he was not then challenged. Speaking at his own press conference on 12 November 1982, with his chief dissenters sitting beside him, Rawlings claimed that there had been no attempted coup but merely a misunderstanding, which had now been resolved. Nevertheless, matters continued to deteriorate within the PNDC until 23 November when another coup was attempted, and the JFM members of the PNDC itself were arrested or forced to flee. From that moment on the JFM became a broken shell, and the NDM and its strategy gained ascendancy.

4 The Ruling Movement

Ghana under the December 31st revolution, has not produced a unified Marxist–Leninist party as a leading force. Instead, a number of Marxist groups came to occupy leading positions in the ruling movement. For the sake of brevity, this movement is referred to as the PNDC, or the December 31st revolution.

Historical Outline of the PNDC

In the early morning hours of 31 December 1981, revolutionary units overthrew President Limann and suspended the 1979 Third Republic's constitution. The Provisional National Defence Council was created on 2 January 1982 as the supreme political authority in Ghana, although its membership, apart from Rawlings, was not officially announced until 11 January 1982 (*Ghanaian Times*, 12 January 1982; *West Africa*, 11 January, 1982, p. 70; PNDC Establishment Proclamation, 11 January 1982). Despite the provision for a maximum of eleven members, only seven were declared to be initial members in the PNDC (Establishment) Proclamation. The members, listed in order of precedence by this proclamation, were: Flight-Lieutenant Jerry John Rawlings (listed curiously as John Jerry) as Chairman, Brigadier Joseph Nunoo-Mensah, the Rev. Dr (Vincent) Kwabena Damuah, Warrant Officer Class One Joseph Adjei Buadi, Sergeant Daniel Aloga Akata-Pore, Joachim Amartey Quaye (also known as Amarte Kwei) and Chris Bukari Atim.

A brief description of the PNDC members is in order here. Rawlings was born in Accra on 22 June 1947. He was a Flight-Lieutenant in the Ghana Air Force until he assumed power, at the age of 28, during the June 4th 1979 insurrection. He received a high school education at the elite Achimota school on the outskirts of Accra before being accepted into the officer training programme in Ghana. He was a daring pilot, continuing to fly while in power both in 1979 and since 1981. He was a popular officer with his men, a somewhat unique quality in the Ghanaian officer corps at that time. He was very interested in sport. He enjoyed horse riding and boxing and he was the Armed Forces boxing officer, frequently assisting Justice Annan, who was the head of Ghanaian amateur boxing, to stack chairs after amateur fights. (Rawlings was instrumental in persuading Justice Annan to join the PNDC in July 1984.) In a society fractured by tribalism, Rawlings is a Ghanaian. Born of a Scottish father and an Ewe mother, he is related through his wife Nana Agyeman to Asante (Ashanti) royalty. Although this fact was not widely known in Ghana, it perhaps symbolizes the desired overcoming of rivalry between the Ewe and Asante. In any case he is a fierce Ghanaian nationalist who is aware of both the potential and the problems of Ghana (interview with Rawlings, Accra, 7 August 1984).

Rawlings' pugnacious patriotism derives from his long-standing moral passion for social justice. As a boy he considered becoming a priest and helping to achieve a morally just society. At another point he considered the idea of forming a Robin Hood-type group that would take from the rich to give to the poor, thus achieving social justice. His public and private attitudes to women also reflect a concern for social justice. He has argued against the traditional customs which deprived widows of family and private property on the death of their husbands (see PNDC draft legislation on the family). A number of the most senior PNDC advisers were women. Rawlings has chided male revolutionaries who leave their passion for social justice at their front doors when dealing with their wives (interview with Rawlings, Accra, 7 August 1984. See chapters 6 and 9 also for a fuller discussion of the PNDC's policy towards women).

Rawlings' sense of social justice was honed by his observation of the governments of General Acheampong, General Akuffo and President Limann, as well as by his experiences in the 1979 AFRC. His participation in Marxist study groups run by the NDM and discussions with the JFM leaders gave his earlier understanding a new analytical context.

Brigadier Joseph Nunoo-Mensah was the second-ranking member of the PNDC. He had a national-democratic orientation. Having gained the respect of many junior ranks, he was appointed Chief of Defence Staff by the AFRC in 1979. He had earlier been fired by

President Limann in a bid to remove 'radical' elements. Nunoo-Mensah's 'unacceptable' qualities were apparently his acceptability to the junior ranks, his honesty and, perhaps the key, the fact that he had been publicly associated with the AFRC. He was reappointed Chief of Defence Staff by Rawlings in his 31st December 1981 broadcast. He resigned on 23 November 1982, eleven months after the start of the December 31st Revolution.

The Rev. Dr Vincent Kwabena Damuah ranked third in the PNDC at the start of the revolution. Damuah was representative of the progressives in the various religious communities. The Christian churches had been very active during 1977 and 1978 in the campaigns to replace General Acheampong's regime. Damuah was a Roman Catholic priest who had come under severe censure from church authorities for his populist views but had been reinstated as a priest in 1980. He resigned on 19 August 1982 from the PNDC and later also from the Roman Catholic church, founding his own 'Afrikanist' religion.

Warrant Officer Class One Joseph Adjei Buadi (also spelt Boadi) was the fourth-ranking member of the PNDC. Buadi, an Akan, had taken part in the June 4th revolution/insurrection. He was a member of the AFRC Secretariat. After 31 December 1981, he was made Co-ordinator, Armed Forces Defence Committees. He resigned from the PNDC in December 1984.

Sergeant Daniel Aloga Akata-Pore was born in 1955 in Koforidua, Eastern Region, but came from the Fra Fra ethnic group of the Upper East Region in the North. He received his secondary education by enlisting in the Boy's Company of the Armed Forces. He rapidly advanced through the ranks to serve as an instructor at the Military Academy and Training School and studied for a B.Sc. in Economics at the University of Cape Coast (*West Africa*, 15 February 1982, p. 429). He was a leading member of the June 4th Movement (JFM). Involved in the attempted coup of October/November 1982, he was arrested and imprisoned until January 1984. On his release he went into exile in Britain.

Joachim Amarte Kwei was the sixth-ranking PNDC member. Kwei had been a trade-union leader and had led the GIHOC (Ghana Industrial Holding Corporation) employees to occupy the parliament

Table 1 Multiple holding of positions in revolutionary, government and mass organizations in Ghana, 1982

Person	PNDC	Movement	Government	Mass organizations
Flt.-Lt. Jerry John Rawlings	Chairman	Chairman, JFM	PNDC Chairman (Head of Government and State)	Chairman, National Defence Committee
Brigadier Joseph Nunoo-Mensah	Member		PNDC member, Chief of Defence Staff	
Rev. Dr Vincent Kwabena Damuah	Member		PNDC member	
W.O.I. Joseph Adjei Buadi	Member		PNDC member	Co-ordinator, Armed Forces Defence Committees
Sgt. Daniel Aloga Akata-Pore	Member	JFM leader	PNDC member	Secretary, Armed Forces Defence Committees
Joachim Amarte Kwei	Member		PNDC member	Trade unions
Chris Bukari Atim	Member	JFM General Secretary	PNDC member	National Defence Committee

buildings during President Limann's regime. Kwei was one of the trade unionists who were dissatisfied with the TUC leadership and he worked to replace it, succeeding in April 1982. In mid-1982, three High Court judges and the GIHOC group personnel manager were murdered. Some suspicion fell on Kwei, as a former GIHOC employee. According to some reports, Kwei had been fired by the GIHOC group personnel manager for his occupation of Parliament, and Kwei had supposedly used his rise to power to settle this old score. Kwei resigned from the PNDC anyway, and was later tried on murder charges and executed on 17 August 1983.

Chris Bukari Atim was the seventh-ranking PNDC member. He was born in 1953 in Gbedema, Sandema District, in the northern Upper East Region. After finishing his high school education at Navrongo Secondary School, he studied Building Technology at the University of Science and Technology in Kumasi. In 1978 he became first national vice-president of the National Union of Ghana Students (NUGS). He was also editor of the radical *A Luta* magazine (*West Africa*, 15 February 1982, p. 429). Atim, as General Secretary of the June Fourth Movement (JFM), was its senior leader after Rawlings, around whom the JFM had been created after Limann purged Rawlings from the military in 1980. Atim was articulate but had limited political experience. He had advocated a quick move to socialism and had hoped to build a power-base from the defence committees that would allow this. Following the attempted coup of October/November 1982, he escaped from Ghana, issued his letter of resignation from the PNDC on 3 December 1982 and made his way to London.

The social and political characteristics of the first generation of the PNDC can be summarized briefly. Four out of the seven members were either currently or formerly military men, the other three civilians. One was a former student, one a priest and one was a trade-union leader. They were youthful. They were all men. They were neither wealthy nor chiefs. All were literate. Three definitely belonged to the JFM. In addition to belonging to the JFM, Rawlings had had a close asociation with the NDM.

The fate of the first generation of the PNDC is indicative of the turbulence to be expected in revolutions. Rawlings, the PNDC Chairman, was the only one of the original seven who stayed in post beyond the third anniversary of the December 31st revolution. In all, three PNDC members resigned—two of them in 1982. Buadi lasted until December 1984, when he also resigned. One member was executed in 1983. Two staged a coup attempt in 1982. By the end of 1982, over half the first generation of PNDC members had left. Like the French Revolution, and the Russian Revolutions of February and October 1917, top leadership changes were rapid and often took dramatic forms—coups and executions.

Before coming to the second and third generations of the PNDC, it is important to examine briefly the causes of the break-up of the first generation in 1982. The major points of contention were the result of conflicts between the left on organizational and policy matters and the ambiguities apparently attendant upon the national-democratic phase of the revolution. The Marxist movements were not unified into one Marxist–Leninist party. Frictions between personalities and movements grew into a state of aggravated irritation which eventually erupted into the tropical ulcer of the coup attempt of October/ November 1982, and the resultant gutting of the June Fourth Movement. While there had been some attempts to unify the left before the revolution overthrew Limann, they had not been successful. There were personality clashes. The movements had competed intensely to seize the ideological high ground and to recruit limited sectors of the population. The JFM leadership was mainly composed of young students and ex-students, while the New Democratic Movement (NDM) drew much of its top leadership from the older professionals, especially university teachers. Thus, at least part of the friction between the two organizations was generational and it reflected tensions that seem to characterize the professor-student relationship. The JFM had become more orientated towards action, while the NDM was very concerned to develop its cadres' knowledge of Marxist–Leninist theory as the precondition to effective action: in short, the two movements had different perceptions about what was necessary and what was possible in Ghana, before the revolution even started.

The beginning of the revolution in fact overrode their differences but did little to resolve them. Despite the small number of effective cadres, the various movements found themselves competing after 31 December 1981 for influence with Rawlings and the rest of the PNDC and for the most important positions in the revolutionary regime. There is nothing inherent in the competition *per se* which would necessarily have led to the sharp split that did in fact occur. The lack of a unified vanguard party did mean that one possible vehicle for the resolution of these differences was lacking, and consequently that there was a lack of coherent leadership among the left. This is a key point for the national-democratic stage of the socialist revolution when progressive, non-socialist forces are part of the leadership grouping, and the potential for the side-lining of socialism is perhaps greatest.

By the time of the October/November attempted coup (discussed in Chapter 7), both movements had entrenched their positions. The JFM occupied positions of power in the PNDC itself and in the network of defence committees, including their guiding body, the NDC. NDM members included the powerful Secretary for Finance, and many of the top advisers around Rawlings. Having placed themselves strategically, members of the movements came into conflict over the direction of the revolution. The JFM wanted to move quickly to consolidate socialism. The NDM argued that, though desirable, this was not possible. The NDM argued that the economic and political preconditions for Marx's socialism had not yet reached the point of popular take-off. In order for this to take place, the NDM argued, economic reconstruction was essential. Like Lenin's New Economic Policy (NEP) in the Soviet Union, private business was to be granted a role in this process. The scale of reconstruction in Ghana required access to foreign public capital.

The PNDC first investigated the socialist countries and Libya as potential sources of capital but they did not have what the PNDC considered sufficient amounts (interview with Dr K. Botchwey, Secretary for Finance, Accra, 8 August 1984). A debate ensued within the government over what should be done. Rawlings, the NDM and the technocrats eventually agreed that the only possible sources of funding were the International Monetary Fund (IMF) and the World Bank. While the NDM were wary of the international institutions, with their reputation as guardians of American business and political interests to the exclusion of all others, the Secretary for Finance believed that if the Ghanaians drew up their own programme of reconstruction and if it was technically well done, then the IMF would have less cause or power to impose its own programme. At any rate, there was no alternative (interview, Accra, 8 August 1984). The June Fourth Movement (JFM) argued that even to negotiate with the IMF and the World Bank signified that the revolution had been betrayed, that socialism was being rolled back and capitalism was being put back in charge (interviews, Accra, June–August 1984).

Tensions within the PNDC were heightened by this debate. The leadership of the JFM felt they had sufficient cause to remove Rawlings and the NDM. They failed in their October/November 1982 attempt, however; the senior members of JFM were forced to flee, were arrested or otherwise neutralized. More fundamental changes occurred within the revolution, however, than the mere removal of a few personalities. The JFM was broken, the leadership left, their newspaper ceased publication for a time. The remnants of the JFM only started to regroup openly by the middle of 1984. The pool of revolutionary cadres sharply decreased at a time when the problems of Ghana were increasing: 1983 saw the return of one million Ghanaians deported from Nigeria, as well as a severe food shortage. The National Defence Committee and its subordinate defence committees came to be seen as a base for the JFM coup attempt. Consequently, a shift in power took place from the JFM to the loyalist NDM, and from the NDC (which was finally abolished at the end of 1984) to Rawlings, his advisers and the PNDC 'cabinet', the ministerial and regional secretaries.

In the aftermath, the second and third generations of the PNDC emerged. By the end of 1982, only Rawlings and Buadi remained from the first generation. Mrs Aanaa Enin, Ebo Tawiah and the Nandom Na, Naa Polkuu Konkuu Chiiri were added to form the second generation PNDC which lasted until mid-1984. Mrs Aanaa Enin and Ebo Tawiah were appointed to the PNDC as replacements for Damuah and Kwei shortly after the latters' resignations in mid-August 1982 (*West Africa*, 23 August 1982, p. 2188).

Enin had been the manager of marketing for the State Fishing Corporation and the first woman on the PNDC. She has spoken frequently on women's issues and on foreign relations. She has further acted as head of state when receiving foreign diplomats. Ebo Tawiah was Secretary-General of the Maritime and Dockworkers Union. Like his predecessor Kwei, he represented organized Labour on the PNDC.

The Nandom Na replaced Sergeant A. Akata-Pore (after his coup attempt and subsequent arrest) and Brigadier-General Nunoo-Mensah (who resigned on 22 November 1982) in early January 1983. The Nandom Na, Naa Polkuu Konkuu Chiiri, was a Northerner, a chief from the Upper West Region. (The region was created just before his appointment to the PNDC.) After his death from illness on 25 August 1984, he was replaced by another Northerner Alhaji Mahama Iddrisu, aged 51. He had been PNDC Secretary for Transport and Communications (*West Africa*, 8 October 1984, p. 2059).

Significantly, by the beginning of 1983, the proportion of soldiers in the PNDC had been reduced by one half. Labour retained a representative on the PNDC, while a female manager member was added, as was a chief—all three were new categories for the PNDC. Essentially, then, the second generation PNDC had expanded its social composition to be more broadly representative. This was compatible with the national democratic strategy.

Similarly the third generation of the PNDC gave a wider social and political representation to act as an opening for more of the national democratic forces of Ghana, but without the traumatic membership changes that occurred in the transition from the first and second PNDCs. In July 1984 Mrs S. Alhassan and Justice D. F. Annan joined the PNDC. Alhassan represented women and the Nkrumahists (she had been a minister in Nkrumah's government). Annan was a retired judge, a farmer and active in Ghana's boxing circles. Before he was appointed to the PNDC, he was due to head Ghana's delegation to the 1984 Olympics in Los Angeles (interview, Accra, 4 August 1984). He was Vice-Chairman of the PNDC.

The PNDC was again expanded in July 1985 when two new members were appointed to the PNDC. Captain Kojo Tsikata (retd.) had previously been the Special Adviser to the PNDC. This post was abolished upon Tsikata's promotion. Instead, he became the PNDC member responsible for foreign affairs and national security. Tsikata, whose family was from the Volta Region, had been active in the youth wing of Nkrumah's Convention People's Party. After becoming an officer in the Ghanaian Army, he was sent in 1960 to the Congo (Zaïre) with Ghana's United Nations contingent. Here he observed the meddling of foreign powers in the Congolese revolution. In 1965

Nkrumah sent him to provide military assistance to the MPLA, the liberation movement fighting for the independence of Angola from Portugal. He maintained his interest in political life (interview, Accra, 1 August 1984).

P. V. Obeng had been a mechanical engineer in a private fishing company, where he eventually became Technical Director of a group of companies. His promotion to the PNDC reinforced his effective position as Prime Minister. His title was expanded to PNDC Co-ordinating Secretary and Chairman of the Committee of PNDC Secretaries (interview, Accra, 1 August 1984; *West Africa*, 22 July 1985, p. 1519).

Towards the end of 1985 two further members were recruited to the PNDC. Major-General Arnold Quainoo, the Force Commander, had been chosen by the junior ranks of the June 4th uprising to be the Force Commander during the AFRC government. Quainoo was fired by the Limann government for being popular with the junior ranks, but Rawlings announced his immediate restoration at the start of the December 31st revolution. Brigadier Mensa-Wood was Commander of the Military Academy and Training School.

The Organizations

The contemporary organized left in Ghana dates from the June 4th 1979 uprising, and its short-lived but turbulent government, the Armed Forces Revolutionary Council (AFRC), which handed over power to President Limann's civilian regime on 24 September 1979. Limann's Third Republic was in turn overthrown on 31 December 1981 by many of the same forces, led by Rawlings, who initiated and participated in the June 4th uprising.

However, the experiences of 1979 to 1981 led to fundamental recasting of revolutionary political forces. Revolutionaries moved from relative isolation into active movements—from study to action. Marxism gained ideological ascendancy. These changes were influenced by a number of factors. The left had realized the relative ease with which state power might be seized when Acheampong's grip had been broken in 1978. The 1979 AFRC government served as an example of what revolutionaries should and should not do when exercising power: the possibility of state power thus dangled like a tempting apple before the left, in contrast to the situation that had existed since Nkrumah's overthrow in 1966.

The possibility of taking power was complemented by the perceived need to seize power. The military governments of General Acheampong (1972–8) and General Akuffo (1978–9), as well as the civilian government of Limann (1979–81), were seen as corrupt and incapable of dealing with the deepening economic crisis. Inflation was rampant, goods were becoming scarcer for all but the wealthy. Limann's Military Intelligence unit harassed certain former revolutionaries, on occasion even threatening their lives. Ideas of possible action fell upon receptive ears. The left grew.

The June Fourth Movement (JFM)

The June Fourth Movement was born in the aftermath of the June 4th uprising in 1979. The insurrection temporarily interrupted the transition to civilian rule which General Akuffo had promised. The main focus of this transition was the imminent national election. The People's Revolutionary Party (PRP) was the main Marxist party wishing to contest the elections (there was also the Commoner's Party). The PRP, however, was hindered by the limiting requirements of the election: it was unable to open the necessary offices in all nine regions and one hundred and forty constituencies.

The PRP became involved in a dispute when Limann's People's National Party (PNP) offered to absorb the PRP. One PRP faction, led by Johnny Hansen, accepted. A 'rejectionist' bloc of the PRP, however, mainly composed of students and workers, led by Zaaya Yeebo, S. Gariba, Kofi Klu and T. Kodwo Ababio-Nubuor (the latter of the People's Revolutionary League of Ghana), refused 'to be part of the tricks and machinations of bourgeois politics' (JFM source, Accra, 1984). Then came the June 4th revolution. The PRP rejectionist elements came into close contact with the ruling AFRC, and its leader, Rawlings. As dissatisfaction grew among the left after the AFRC had handed over power to Limann, the June Fourth Movement emerged under the chairmanship of Rawlings.

The JFM was to be cast in the mould of a mass movement, guided by Marxism, suited to the national democratic phase of the socialist revolution. The JFM members were mainly young: students, youths, workers and soldiers. Membership and sympathizers together numbered a few thousand. The *Workers' Banner* was the JFM newspaper.

The leaders of the JFM included Rawlings (Chairman, former AFRC chairman, PNDC chairman), Kwasi Adu (President), Nicholas Atampugre, Nyeya Yen, S. Gariba (former PRP), Zaaya Yeebo (former PRP), Sergeant Daniel Aloga Akata-Pore, and Rudolf Amenga. They were nearly all recent university graduates or university student leaders and activists who had played supportive roles in the June 4th uprising. They were young—many of them in their twenties. Most came from the Upper and Northern Regions. These demographic considerations contributed to the JFM's advances in the Upper West and Upper East Regions and with northerners in the military. One JFM source also believed that the regional roots of the JFM contributed to tensions with such southern-initiated organizations as the New Democratic Movement.

The JFM stated that it was 'a mass national democratic movement committed to the realization of true democracy and fulfilment of aspirations of the mass of Ghanaian peoples'. Its goal went beyond the achievement of parliamentary democracy (bourgeois democracy) to the accomplishment of Marx's social, economic and political democracy. Anti-imperialist, anti-colonialist and pro-working class in orientation, the JFM argued that Ghana's economic crisis was caused by underdevelopment (i.e. a distinctive distortion of economic processes characterized by the export of resources, the growth of enclaves of local business dependent on foreign business and the stagnation or very slow growth of economic benefits for the majority of the population).

This underdevelopment was seen to be rooted in the colonial regime's selfish exploitation of Ghana's natural resources. Moreover, this process was carried over into the political realm. Most people continued to suffer from imperialism after the granting of formal political independence as they did to a similar degree under colonialism. The only way out of the situation is to fight imperialism through revolutionary, and ultimately socialist, means. (This conceptualization reflects the influences of the work of Franz Fanon. See especially his

The Wretched of the Earth.) The JFM argued that under neo-colonialism (i.e. formal constitutional independence but *de facto* economic and political subordination to imperialism: see Nkrumah's *Neocolonialism*, which became influential among the Ghanaian left) imperialism and its Ghanaian agents robbed the country, while 'the working people continue to suffer ignorance and unemployment, their children suffered illiteracy, hunger and neglect. It [neo-colonialism] means that the children of these working people were condemned to the fate of their fathers: that of ignorance, exploitation and unemployment.'

Another significant point in the JFM's analysis of Ghana was their argument that, since independence, only the Nkrumah government (1957–66) and the AFRC (4 June–24 September 1979) had been interested in the fate of workers, peasants and soldiers. Nkrumah was believed to have marginally improved the material conditions of working people. The AFRC was seen as a real blow to imperialism because it attacked some of the handmaidens of imperialism. All the other military and civilian governments, excepting Nkrumah and the AFRC, were seen as being responsible for the decline in the power and standard of living of workers and peasants in Ghana.

The JFM took its name from the June 4th 1979 uprising precisely because it represented a high point in resistance to imperialism and hence in its potential for emancipating the people of Ghana. The JFM argued:

To every oppression, there is resistance. It is in fulfilment of this natural law that the working people of this country have resisted by various means the exploitation they have been subjected to. That was what gave rise to the glorious June 4 uprising which sparked off among the lower ranks of the Armed Forces and immediately received the overwhelming support among the working populations. For the three months that the AFRC were in power, international finance capital and its local agents were terrified.

A third important part of the JFM's analysis of Ghana was their critique of 'bourgeois democracy' and their consequent desire to achieve 'popular Democracy'. The JFM rejected forms of 'democracy' that effectively limited the possibility of being elected to the wealthy minority. This was the basic fault in Ghana's Third Republic which produced the Limann government. Hence the JFM did not accept it as legitimate—a true democracy. Electoral politics did not of itself mean true democracy. The JFM stated that the Limann (1979–81) and Busia (1969–72) governments meant that the 'working masses' only received the right to vote every four or five years for the representatives of the rich who entered government in order to enrich themselves. (Not since Nkrumah have there been two successive administrations elected to power. Following Nkrumah, both elected administrations had their first term interrupted by a coup.) True democracy meant rule by the majority of the people (that is, workers and peasants) and not effective domination by the wealthy few. The JFM reasoned that 'it is only when the working people control the affairs of the state that one can say that democracy has been achieved.' Developing their Marxist democratic focus, the JFM stated that 'the emancipation of the working class is therefore the principal preoccupation of the JFM.' hence, the JFM initially received the December 31st 1981 Revolution with great enthusiasm.

The JFM had a socialist economic policy: all the means of production were to be owned collectively (either by the state or by private cooperatives). Reflecting the agrarian economic base of the country and its people, the JFM was especially concerned with the question of the collectivization of agriculture and land. They rejected the prevailing mixed system of traditional, private and state control and/or ownership of land. They believed that while chiefs and others were supposed to control land in trust for their kin or group and thus share any land benefits, the chiefs were in fact only enriching themselves from the tribute and royalties generated by these land rights. Accordingly, the JFM called for 'the establishment of collective farms whenever possible as a way of instilling the spirit of collectivity into the people and also as a way of showing that they can achieve maximum yields by pooling their resources together'. Farmers were to be mobilized to take back land owned by absentee landlords.

Privately controlled industry and trade were to be collectivized, using the mechanisms of state-controlled or co-operative stores and shops (People's Shops were established after 31 December 1981) and state-owned factories. With regard to public transport and goods transportation, all vehicles, except taxis, were to be nationalized. The JFM argued that state-owned companies would operate much more efficiently once the deliberate sabotage of these corporations by jealous wealthy businessmen had been stopped. These men sought to prevent competition by the state and were anxious to ensure that socialism could not compete with private-sector business. Bribery of officials by the wealthy was thought to account for the manipulation of import allocations, which went against the state corporations.

In terms of social services, the JFM advocated universal and free access to education (from primary school to university), medical care and legal services. Private medical practice was to be abolished since it discriminated against the poor who could not afford it. Social services were to serve working people. These policies were significant since they represented a reorientation away from the professional classes who derived their incomes either by selling their services privately or by charging illegal private fees at government facilities (at some hospitals doctors routinely demanded bribes, ranging from the equivalent of one to five months of an ordinary worker's wages). This aspect of the JFM's programme therefore constituted a political challenge to one of the most politically active classes in Ghana.

Writing during the Limann era, before the outbreak of the revolution, the JFM confirmed that it wished to become a Bolshevik-style party that would lead a successful revolution: 'our long-term objective is the formation of an authentic working-class political party to wrestle political power for the realization of the aspirations and protection of the interests of the working people.'

In the process of building this Marxist–Leninist vanguard party, certain tasks were of key importance. The JFM had to be in the frontline of the fight for political and economic democracy for the whole people, but especially for the workers. Accordingly, the JFM had to integrate itself into the working class and to lead its struggle. As a corollary to this, the JFM could develop winning strategies for the workers only by unifying the working class, farmers, progressive professionals and business people as well as other national democratic elements in the fight against imperialism and its local agents.

In the period leading up to the formation of the December 31st revolution, the JFM concentrated its energies in four fields of endeavour: production, adult education, political eduction and political action. During 1980 the JFM established farms in a number of regions. These were to provide employment for the unemployed and to act as pilot projects for testing and demonstrating a revolutionary lifestyle to other Ghanaians. One of these farms became famous when in 1981 the Limann government accused Rawlings of using it to train future revolutionaries in the use of weapons. (Rawlings overthrew Limann that same year.) The farms in fact did sell their produce. This policy of providing for the economic welfare of some members is similar to that of the earlier African Youth Command (AYC).

Again, responding to a social need, the JFM provided educational opportunities for adults and youth of the poorer sections of the community. The JFM provided free classes at Labone Secondary School in Accra for the illiterate and for those who wanted to complete their 'O' and 'A' levels for the General Certificate of Education. Thus, the JFM was able to broaden its contacts with those who had cause to be dissatisfied with the state system's handling of public education. The contrast was stark: the state system was becoming more and more paralysed as it was denied funding: the children of workers and peasants received a very inferior education, while the private schools which only the wealthy could afford did well. The JFM used the social background of its members to benefit workers and young people alike. Under these conditions, it was made quite clear to those taking part in the classes who it was who had their interests at heart—the JFM and not the rich.

The JFM conducted political education by means of public and private meetings, by publicizing its disagreements with the Limann government, and by publishing its own newspapers. Public meetings were organized around days of political significance to the nation (such as 4 June, independence day) or to the JFM (i.e. the opening of a new branch). Major speakers at these meetings included Rawlings (Chairman of the JFM and later the PNDC), Father Damuah (Ghanaian Roman Catholic Priest and later a PNDC member) and Father Visser (a Roman Catholic priest from Holland, then stationed in the Madina suburb of Accra).

The JFM made public campaigns out of its differences with the Limann government. One major focus was the perceived attempt by the Limann government to help undermine the sentences of the AFRC. Numerous wealthy individuals had been convicted of various charges of corruption and were consequently given long prison sentences, fined large sums of money and/or had had their property confiscated. The JFM movement accused the Limann government of trying to overturn these AFRC sentences. This enabled the JFM to explain its opposition to the Limann government and to the wealthy who backed it. Another major campaign waged by the JFM was the protection of Captain Kojo Tsikata (retired, later PNDC member) from the surveillance, harassment and even attempted murder by Limann's Military Intelligence.

Besides publishing its own pamphlets, the JFM also had its own national newspaper, *Workers' Banner*, with a special edition, *Kpano* for the Upper and Northern regions. These ceased publication after some of the JFM leaders were involved in the October/November 1982 coup attempt.

The JFM had a reputation in some circles for placing more emphasis on action than on internal theoretical education. Besides the economic, educational and publicity campaigns, the JFM also took part in a number of strikes and demonstrations by workers and students as a means of promoting their demands during a period of ruinous inflation and their contact with the JFM. Perhaps the most significant strike and demonstration led by the JFM was the one which resulted in the temporary occupation of Parliament. J. Amarte Kwei (later a PNDC member) was the union leader of the Ghana Industrial Holding Corporation (GIHOC, a state-owned company). The GIHOC workers forced their way into Parliament, ate a meal prepared for the MPs, and occupied the building until the workers were forced out. They were later fired, and only reinstated after the PNDC had seized power. The final political act of the JFM during President Limann's period of office was to take part in seizing power from Limann's hands on 31 December 1981. Thereafter, the JFM participated in the process of conducting the revolution.

By the time the December 31st revolution began, the JFM had become the largest of the revolutionary movements (the AYC remained a special case because of its official stand that it did not become involved in 'domestic' politics). The JFM had grown in certain areas of the Upper, Northern, Eastern and Greater Accra regions, but did not yet have a truly national network. Had there been more time before the revolution began, the JFM would probably have achieved that status.

Certainly, the JFM was able to command a significant number of top positions once the revolution started. For example, three, possibly four, members of the PNDC were also members of the JFM (Rawlings, Akata-Pore and Atim; there is some doubt as to Kwei's affiliation). Zaaya Yeebo was Secretary for Youth and Sports. Kwasi Adu was Chairman of the new revolutionary youth group, the Democratic Youth League of Ghana (DYLG). Other senior JFM leaders such as Nicholas Atampugre, Nyeya Yen and Rudolf Amenga were in the upper levels of the National Defence Committee. However, the JFM's influence was broken in the aftermath of the October–November coup attempt by leaders of the JFM and the People's Revolutionary League of Ghana.

The People's Revolutionary League of Ghana (The League)

The People's Revolutionary League of Ghana was formed by elements of the PRP who rejected the PRP's absorption by Limann's PNP. The League grew out of the student ferment that took place after the 4 June 1979 uprising. Their role was reminiscent of the role that students such as Mao had played during the 1911 Revolution. Student participation increased as the students left their schools and campuses for the holidays, which began a month after 4 June. Accordingly, the left decided to try to use this opportunity to organize the students.

During this period of the AFRC, in particular July/August 1979, students were mobilized on the basis of patriotism and community service. As a result, they took part in a number of voluntary projects, such as transporting cocoa and labouring on community sanitation works. High school and college and university students worked together on these projects. The League was founded by T. Kodwo Ababio-Nubuor from among a number of the students temporarily encamped at Achimota College (on the outskirts of Accra near the University of Ghana). The leadership of the League included Ababio-Nubuor (General Secretary), George Quaynor-Mettle and Ali Yemoh.

The former had studied history and philosophy at the University of Ghana. After graduation, he taught at Apam Secondary School, Central Region. Membership of the League was small and located mainly in the Mamprobi area of Accra until 31 December 1981.

Like the JFM, the League was Marxist in orientation, policy and ideology. It placed emphasis on attempting to organize students, young people and workers against imperialism and in aid of national democracy. It organized public rallies, discussions, voluntary work and the distribution of leaflets. Like the JFM, the League was critical of the New Democratic Movement (NDM) for supposedly being too theoretical and not sufficiently active in its revolutionary work.

Once the December 31st revolution had started, the League formed a United Front with the JFM. They both became increasingly critical of Rawlings, the PNDC and the NDM, accusing them of betraying the revolution. On 29 October 1981, at a meeting of the leaders of the Accra Region people's defence committees and the worker's defence committees, the leader of the League announced that Rawlings had been deposed and a JFM leader, Sergeant Akata-Pore, had become PNDC Chairman. The League leader, Ababio–Nubuor, fled into exile when he saw his plans had not materialized. This signalled the demise of the old League (the United Front, and indeed the old JFM), although George Quaynor–Mettle remained and retained his influential position in the December 31st revolution as under-Secretary for the Greater Accra Region.

The New Democratic Movement (NDM)

The New Democratic Movement (NDM) was founded in Accra on May Day, 1 May, 1980, the day symbolic of working-class struggle around the world. The NDM was a Marxist–Leninist vanguard organization that operated in a national democratic and anti-imperialist context.

At its inaugural meeting, the NDM featured two speakers: Abraham Dodoo (the NDM's Chairman) and Dr Ebo Hutchful, a political science lecturer at the University of Ghana. Dodoo, a civil servant, focused on the reasons for the establishment of the NDM. Existing political parties were criticized as being undemocratic—mere playthings of the rich: businessmen, lawyers, priests and intellectuals. The NDM was to be a vehicle that would allow true participation and mobilization of the masses. This was essential if the economic crisis was to be overcome. Dodoo said, 'All we are seeking to do is to mobilize all those who love Mother Ghana, irrespective of party affiliation, religion or creed, to join us to pool our resources and energies together to discuss the issues facing Ghana and suggest solutions for them.' (*West Africa*, 19 May 1980, pp. 898–9.) Accordingly, the NDM's immediate task was to organize events that would contribute to these processes of analysis and consensus-building as the necessary building blocks for effective action. This involved talks and other forms of political education, community work and (reflecting the social composition of the NDM's leadership) the provision of legal aid.

Hutchful focused on a theme that he was to propound in other forums (including the 1981 Calgary conference of the Canadian Association of African Studies) and which, given what the NDM's position would be in three years' time, had a certain unintentional irony. His theme was 'Foreign Debts and National Development'. He argued that the government of Ghana should not accept loans from the World Bank and the IMF since these loans would allow international capitalism, through the medium of the IMF and the World Bank, to gain control over Ghana's economic politics. Moreover, this would not solve Ghana's economic problems but merely place them in the hands of the perpetuators of those problems. Ghanaians must rely on themselves to solve Ghana's economic crisis (*West Africa*, 19 May 1980, p. 899).

Three years later, having assumed power, an NDM leader became Secretary for Finance. He was forced, by necessity and lack of alternatives, to negotiate a loan package with the IMF and the World Bank, but he maintained the concern, expressed earlier by Hutchful, not to surrender Ghana's economy to the IMF and the World Bank (interview with Dr Kwesi Botchwey, Accra, 8 August 1984).

Most of the leadership was drawn from the professoriate and professionals of the Accra area. They came to occupy many key leadership positions in the revolution. Prior to 31 December 1981 the NDM concentrated on political education of their members and other citizens as well as recruiting and publishing their journal, *Direction*.

NDM membership was largely drawn from university professors and students at the University of Ghana, at Legon, which is on the outskirts of Accra. By contrast, the JFM had recruited students from the University of Cape Coast as well as some from the University of Ghana.

Both the NDM and JFM were constrained by the lack of time between their foundation and the start of the December 31st revolution. Starting with a few individuals, a particular regional pattern of recruitment began to emerge. Often friend recruited friend, and since both usually came from the same region, initial recruiting advances reflected these regional patterns. If there had been sufficient time for these organizations to mature before the revolution started, most likely they would have had regionally-balanced leadership and membership structures. The start of the revolution, however, 'froze' their growth. The implication of this is that, at the start of the revolution, the NDM was seen as a 'southern' organization and the JFM was seen as a 'northern' organization. This does not seem to be an accurate or fair evaluation of how the leadership of these organizations saw themselves, but since others thought that regionalism was present, it did contribute to tensions between them. Other tensions involved personalities and professor–student generational difficulties. Yet the NDM and the JFM were in fact rather similar. Both were Marxist–Leninist. Both were nationalist, Nkrumahist and anti-imperialist. They both believed that Ghana was in the national democratic phase of the socialist revolution. Yet ultimately they differed over what this meant: the 'induced birth' of 'socialism', as in Poland and Afghanistan, or the longer route of Mao's New Democracy.

Nominally, both believed that in the national democratic phase of the Ghanaian revolution, capitalist control over the economy should be eliminated. Judging by the JFM's actions after 31 December 1981, the JFM believed that this should be accomplished quickly, and little allowance was made for the possible contribution that private Ghanaian and foreign capital could make to Ghana's economic recovery. The NDM argued that while a nationwide party was being built up, and given the economic chaos that prevailed in Ghana, a forced march to socialism was not possible. A Pyrrhic victory would alone result unless those two conditions had been met. Both of these entailed mobilizing resources wherever possible. After all, the Soviet Union had made an alliance with such imperialist powers as Britain and the United States in order to defeat fascism, despite the fact that both had sent armies against the Soviet Union at its inception. So the NDM's logic was one of selection.

Before the revolution began, therefore, the NDM argued that what was possible and what was necessary with regard to the economy was 'a gradual and systematic curbing of the control that foreign companies had over our [Ghanaian] economy, especially the blatantly parasitic ones—banking, foreign and international trade, petroleum companies, e.g. B.P., Shell, Texaco, etc., and the assertion of a greater national control over our resources.' The JFM was critical of this selective approach, wishing to launch a full-scale assault on all sectors of foreign and domestic private capital.

Needless to say, the JFM was outraged when the NDM decided after the start of the revolution that, heretical as it might seem, there were valid reasons and precedents (including Lenin's NEP) for accepting foreign investment and loans from the IMF. Capitalism, having contributed to Ghana's economic chaos was to be selectively used to provide a reinvigorated economy that would form the basis for socialism (NDM interviews, May–August 1984). This would seem to be part of an emerging pattern of African Marxism most interestingly demonstrated by the troops of communist Cuba and Angola guarding the oil-producing installations of the American capitalist Gulf Oil company in Angola against attacks instigated by the forces of imperialism in the form of the United States, South Africa, and Zaïre.

The NDM also argued for the renegotiation of agreements with foreign companies that would result in more favourable terms for Ghana. For example, after 31 December 1981, the PNDC opened negotiations with the American aluminium consortium operating Valco in Ghana on the terms of the original unfavourable agreement that Nkrumah had signed. The NDM also advocated that the state should 'gradually take over the major spheres' of industry. In line with the NDM's general national democratic strategy, public and private Ghanaian industries were to be protected against external pressures wherever possible.

With regard to agriculture, the sector of the economy which

absorbs the energies of most Ghanaians, the NDM reflected Mao's line in their concern for the rural poor, especially land-short and landless peasants and agricultural workers. For the NDM, 'some steps need to be taken to make land more easily accessible to the peasantry, in particular the poor landless peasants, thereby clipping the wings of landlordism'. The NDM's caution in advocating a policy on this question reflected their need to establish firm contacts with a rural base. The JFM, for the purpose of contrast alone, argued for the nationalization of all land, even land under traditional tenure, by the state. How this would have been enforced, given the lack of a developed revolutionary base in the countryside, is open to question: certainly the measures proposed by both the NDM and the JFM would have entailed considerable social change in the countryside. The desirability of these measures is beyond the scope of this work. Certainly they could have generated considerable support for the revolution if they had been implemented in a particular manner in those areas of the north where 'foreign' aristocracies extracted tribute from 'local' farmers.

Since the start of the December 31st revolution, the NDM has expanded its organization and political standing. The NDM expanded from its initial base of several hundred at the University of Ghana to other areas of Accra. After 31 December 1981 the NDM was able to set up branches beyond Accra among the working class in the industrial part of Tema, the port of Sekondi-Takoradi and mining towns such as Tarkwa. The membership numbered a few thousand.

The NDM grew in political importance for several reasons. It had a better appreciation of what was possible since it understood better the need for a long-term national democratic strategy, like that of Mao, once the revolution had been prematurely begun. Like the JFM leaders, the NDM leaders shared a special relationship with Rawlings. Unlike the JFM, the NDM was able to exercise patience and did not attempt a coup against Rawlings. Over time, the NDM was able to outstrip the political forerunner, the JFM, gaining influence within the government and in organizational terms once the JFM failed to oust Rawlings.

The African Youth Command (AYC)

The African Youth Command was set up in 1978 in order to further African unity. Its leadership is Pan-African, anti-imperialist and socialist in orientation. The AYC was created as a youth (i.e. 7 to 50 years of age) organization as a result of the Organization of African Unity meeting in Accra. As a promoter of continental unity, it has declared itself to be non-partisan in character, and capable of existing under any government. The AYC has affiliations with several other counterparts in West Africa, most notably Nigeria, Togo, Sierra Leone, Ivory Coast, Liberia, Gambia and Senegal (AYC interview, Accra, 19 June 1984). It is recognized by the OAU, and AYC members regularly use their membership cards as passports to cross West African borders.

The AYC's activities are of two kinds—domestic and international. Internationally, the AYC's first concern is to promote African unity. Accordingly, in recent years the AYC has been active in educating and organizing Ghanaians against apartheid in South Africa and Namibia. The AYC has been one of the major organizers of events such as Soweto Day, which promotes the freedom of Africans in South Africa. This support is based on the pan-African assumption that such freedom from colonial rule is the necessary precondition for a unified free continent. The AYC tries to develop contacts betwen young people in various African countries, as well as with anti-imperialist youth elsewhere—by means of visits, conferences and correspondence. The AYC also sends delegations to conferences of the World Federation of Democratic Youth.

These international concerns also have their domestic aspects. The fight against imperialism, neo-colonialism and racism and for African unity and freedom is carried on through public meetings and articles in the AYC's paper, *The Command*. Selected AYC members, especially from rural areas, have been sent overseas to further their education. Besides education, the AYC has addressed other concerns of young people, such as sport and unemployment. In order to provide at least some young people with skill training and employment opportunities, the AYC established a series of palm oil plantations, farms and bakeries, transport and tailoring co-operatives in the south and central region of the country.

The AYC has the largest and most widespread membership of any left movement in Ghana. In the decade since its foundation, some 600,000 members are reported to have joined the continental organization, while some 20,000 to 30,000 Ghanaians are classified as being active members. Certainly, AYC signs can be observed in many cities, towns and villages of Ghana. AYC members are drawn from a wide range of society: students, peasants, lawyers, workers (including trade union leaders) and others. Dr F. W. A. Akuffo, a medical doctor in Tema, is President of the AYC (Ghana). S. S. Baffuor-Awuah is the Ghana National Secretary and Continental Deputy Secretary-General of the AYC. Having come out in support of the December 31st revolution, a number of AYC leaders have accepted positions of leadership such as secretaries and under-secretaries.

The Movement for Peace and Democracy (MOPAD)

The Movement for Peace and Democracy (MOPAD) worked with the AYC on issues of mutual interest, such as their concern to promote peace and African unity by ending the civil war in Chad (see, for example, their joint declaration to the OAU, dated 11 June 1982). Founded in 1980 during the aftermath of the June 4th radicalization, MOPAD is an anti-imperialist peace group. Using films, lectures, public meetings and other forums such as the mass media, MOPAD has conducted public education on peace, arms control agreements, the struggle against neo-colonialism and apartheid in countries like South Africa, Namibia and the Middle East. MOPAD has not applied itself to domestic issues.

Many of its leaders belong to other organizations, like the AYC, which approximate to a more uniform structure such as a political party. MOPAD leaders occupied senior PNDC leadership posts in administration, the government-owned *Daily Graphic*, and security organizations. They were largely drawn from the student movement: Gyan-Appenteng, Foreign Editor of the *Daily Graphic*, was President of the All-African Students Union, the continental confederation of national student unions. H. P. Akrofi had been President of the National Union of Ghana Students (NUGS) while an undergraduate at the University of Science and Technology (UST) in Kumasi. Steve Akuffo had been President of the UST Student Representative Council. The General Secretary of MOPAD, Kofi Totobi Quakyi (PNDC Deputy Secretary for Information) had risen from being an undergraduate at the University of Cape Coast to being President of NUGS. Following the 31 December revolution, MOPAD's limited membership was absorbed into administrative positions and the organization's independent political life was greatly diminished.

Kwame Nkrumah Revolutionary Guards (KNRG)

The Kwame Nkrumah Revolutionary Guards were founded on 21 September 1980, the anniversary of Kwame Nkrumah's birthday, by former CPP elements who were dissatisfied with the direction that the Limann government was taking. Both the events leading to its foundation and the name of the organization encapsulate Ghana's political history since the 1950s.

Kwame Nkrumah (1909–72), was the nationalist leader who organized the Convention People's Party (CPP) in 1949, and led Ghana to independence from British rule in 1957. During his rule, Nkrumah gradually developed an ideological mixture which included nationalism, Pan-Africanism and 'scientific socialism' that was known as Nkrumahism. After his overthrow in 1966 by right-wing officers, he more clearly accepted and used Marxism–Leninism in his political analysis of Africa. However, from its inception, the CPP contained both capitalist and proto-socialist elements. By 1979 both these elements had momentarily regrouped around the newly-created PNP of Limann in readiness for the transition to civilian rule. One set of left-wing Nkrumahists led by Johnny Hansen, after finding in 1979 that the electoral regulations shackled their PRP, decided to join the PNP in the hope of pushing that party to the left, i.e. to implement its proposed policies. Disappointed by the refusal of Limann and the PNP's financial barons to do so, these left-wing elements formed the KNRG a year later, in 1980, as a 'ginger group' to attempt once more to guide the PNP into Nkrumahist socialism. Frustrated once again by the refusal of the Limann government to move, the KNRG welcomed and supported the December 31st revolution (interview with H. S. T. Provençal, General Secretary, KNRG, Accra, 27 July 1984).

The KNRG were a well-organized movement with branch offices in the seven southern regions by 1984. The KNRG have concentrated on public education and influencing policy rather than trying to take power themselves. Special attention has been paid to organizing labour, youth and farmers. A number of leaders have participated in the government of the revolution. Johnny Hansen, Acting National Chairman of the KNRG, was PNDC Secretary of the Interior. F. A. Jantuah was the Ashanti Regional Secretary. C. S. Takyi was the Brong Ahafo Regional Secretary.

Other Left Movements

The African Youth Brigade was formed as a result of a split within the AYC. The AYB is a 'national democratic' youth movement of perhaps two thousand members (mainly from secondary schools) in the Volta, Brong Ahafo and Greater Accra Regions. It has focused its activities on community self-help projects. The National Secretary was Kwabla Davour and its Patron, Dr M. M. Owusu-Ansah. The Ghana Peace and Solidarity Council was an 'organization of organizations' (of which the AYC was a member). The Council has participated in events promoting peace and the liberation of South Africa. The Movement on National Affairs (MONAS) was active during the Limann period. It organized among students and soldiers, but some of its leaders were jailed after 31 December and the organization came to an end. The Socialist Revolutionary Youth League of Ghana (SRYLOG) is also no longer active.

The Flow of Forces

During the course of the December 31st revolution in Ghana there have been shifts in political emphasis among the different socialist organizations. MONAS, SRYLOG and the old JFM have effectively disappeared: only a remnant of the JFM was left after the 1982 coup

Table 2 Major left organizations, 1982

Organization	Date of foundation	Membership (est.)	Principal leader
June Fourth Movement (JFM)	1980	1,000	Kwasi Adu (President)
People's Revolutionary League of Ghana (PRLG)	1979	100	T. Kodwo Ababio-Nubuor (General Secretary)
New Democratic Movement (NDM)	1980	300	Abraham Dodoo (Chairman)
African Youth Command (AYC)	1974	20,000	Dr F.W.A. Akuffo (President)
Movement for Peace and Democracy (MOPAD)	1980	100	Kofi Quakyi (General Secretary)
Kwame Nkrumah Revolutionary Guards (KNRG)	1980	2,000	H.S.T. (Sonny) Provencal (General Secretary)

attempt. The JFM was eclipsed by the NDM in terms of influencing the PNDC. The AYC and KNRG gained limited access to power within the PNDC, but a Marxist–Leninist vanguard party which could have unified the left never emerged.

5   Revolutionary Tasks and Structures

The revolutionary strategy that had emerged by the end of 1982 combined elements of Lenin's NEP and Mao's 'new democracy'. It had a double thrust. Economically, the goal was to stop the decay, stabilize the economy, and eventually induce positive economic growth (interview with Dr Kwesi Botchwey, Secretary for Finance, 8 August 1984, Accra). Politically, the goal was to create structures that would facilitate the participation of the people in the exercise of power (interview with Flight-Lieutenant J. J. Rawlings, 7 August 1984, Accra). The aims and tone of the revolutionary tasks were aptly summarized in the last paragraph of the PNDC's policy preamble:

> The policies projected under the December 31st Revolution should bear the characteristics of a genuine National Democratic Revolution: They must be anti-imperialist, anti-neo-colonialist and must aim at instituting a popular democracy. These policies must at all times ensure that the national interest is supreme [PNDC, *Preamble*, 1982, p. 8.]

Thus the tasks of the revolution had moved beyond the bourgeois democratic phase to that of national democracy—the building of socialism.

In the early days of the revolution, economic reconstruction was approached in an eclectic, radical rather than a necessarily consistent socialist fashion. The basic economic question faced by the new regime was: should Ghana's shattered economy be reformed or transformed? Those who argued that the real problem was the corruption of capitalism argued for its reform, starting *inter alia* with radical measures to stamp out corruption. These measures were also proposed and supported by those with little knowledge of either capitalism or socialism (as had been the case in the AFRC's destruction of market buildings in Accra and Tamale in 1979), by those wishing to neutralize the leaders and supporters of the previous regime, and by those socialists who wished to strike an early blow against the various constructions of the local allies of international capital.

On the basis of these different understandings, the revolutionaries moved quickly against those suspected of corruption. The cars and assets of the old political parties were seized (*Ghanaian Times*, 5 January 1982), thus effectively neutralizing the coordination of the old regime that existed outside parliament. The freezing of bank accounts and other assets of those suspected of corruption began (*Ghanaian Times*, 4 January 1982). Suspected profiteers, i.e. those making illegal or excessive profits, such as landlords, transport owners and marketeers, were ordered to reduce their prices to the 'control prices' set by the PNDC (for example, *Ghanaian Times*, 2 January 1982).

A variety of bodies were set up to root out corruption. Public tribunals were established to overcome the abuses of the old judicial system and to enforce the new system of price controls. They were to be independent of the 'old' judicial system (PNDC 'Establishment Proclamation, 1981', 11 January 1982, Section 10). The Citizens' Vetting Committee (CVC, renamed in 1984 the Office of the Revenue Commissioners) was established to 'investigate persons whose life styles and expenditures substantially exceeded their known or declared incomes' and related matters (PNDC Law No. 1, Section 4). The CVC was a major instrument for investigating the lifestyle of the wealthy, especially the large-scale traders and professionals generally. Many of these people were shown to have engaged in corruption, and tax evasion in particular. Between its establishment in February 1982 and November 1983, CVC action directly resulted in the collection of 166.3 million Cedis, out of an assessed 306 million Cedis. The increase of almost 500 per cent in taxes paid by the self-employed between 1980 and 1982 has been attributed to the fear on the part of the self-employed of being caught by the CVC (PNDC, *Two Years*, 1984, p. 16).

The National Investigation Committee (PNDC Law No. 2, 2 February 1982) investigated corruption in public office, and the office of the Special Public Prosecuter was responsible for prosecutions arising from these investigations. Under a rather unusual provision, those being investigated by the National Investigations Committee (NIC) had the right to confess and offer 'reparation' to the state in atonement for their crimes (PNDC Law No. 2, Section 8). The PNDC reported that the NIC collected over 5 million Cedis in reparations in the first twenty-two months of the revolution.

In a further effort to end the corruption that had been damaging the economy, anti-smuggling measures were supposed to be tightened around Ghana's borders and at the Kotoka International Airport in Accra. As Ghana's economy collapsed, smuggling had increased. Not surprisingly, it has been difficult to gauge precisely the value of the goods smuggled in and out of the country. Some preliminary estimates indicate that considerable amounts of cocoa, gold, food, timber, marijuana, Ghanaian manufactured goods and Ghanaian currency were smuggled out and significant amounts of consumer goods and foreign currency were illegally brought into the country (Oquaye, 1980, pp. 19, 50-1; Chazan, 1983, pp. 194-5). By the end of the Limann government, something like one half of Ghana's gold production had disappeared! The reasons for this ranged from decreases in productivity due to equipment breakdown, to smuggling.

The success of these measures in revitalizing the economy by recouping government revenues and slowing down illegal if sometimes bizarre flight of capital and goods should not be exaggerated. By 1982, when the PNDC gained power, the Ghanaian state had lost much if not most of its ability to act (Chazan, 1983). By 1984, smuggling was still a significant problem on the borders, but increased security appeared to have reduced the problem at the airport. These policy initiatives, while important in attempting to curb corruption, were of minor significance compared to the overriding economic problems of where to find the capital necessary to repair and rebuild the decayed infrastructure and production capacity of the country. What was needed was far beyond what was available in Ghana.

The Marxist leadership of the revolution became fractured by the vexed question of sources of external funding and the means of using the capital inflow. Initially, both the NDM and the JFM had rejected sources such as the International Monetary Fund (IMF) and the World Bank as being imperialist and therefore hostile to this anti-imperialist revolution (Ahiakpor, 1985; PNDC, *Preamble*, 1982; Checole, 1982). One source believed that, given the composition of the leadership, 'the eventual acceptance of an IMF package therefore remains a possible, if somewhat unlikely scenario' (Jeffries, 1982, p. 316). For socialists even to suggest the acceptance of loans from the IMF and the World Bank has long been sufficient to brand them as 'heretics' at best and counter-revolutionaries at worst. One may imagine the discord among the revolutionary leadership created by the proposal to seek loans from these sources.

The Secretary for Finance, Dr Kwesi Botchwey, argued that loans from these sources could be justified on several grounds. The first stage of Ghana's economic recovery depended on increasing exports such as cocoa, gold and timber. These would provide Ghana with its own independent sources of foreign exchange, which could in turn be used to buy much needed imports such as medicine and machinery. But before this could be done, the roads and railways had to be recon-structed to enable the income-generating exports to get to the ports and thence to their markets.

The 'Socialist' countries and Libya, as mentioned earlier, had been unable to supply the sizable quantity of capital needed. The only alternatives open were the IMF and the World Bank. Ghana was a paying member of these organizations and was therefore entitled to draw capital loans from them. The Ghanaians designed a plan to utilize the proposed loans, whereby they would forestall attempts by the IMF and the World Bank to dictate conditions to them. Dr Botchwey argued that the Ghanaian application was technically so well-designed that the World Bank and the IMF approved it on the basis of merit rather than the political complexion of the PNDC. The PNDC was not surrendering to imperialism (interview, with Dr Botchwey, Secretary for Finance, Accra, 8 August 1984). Others did not necessarily see loans in this light.

The June Fourth Movement denounced the negotiations with the IMF and the World Bank. It summarized its arguments in an editorial in its paper, *The Workers' Banner* (16–23 September 1982). The IMF was characterized as being 'this financial monster, the mercenary head-quarters of imperialist monopoly companies', whose main aims were 'to squeeze our finances, sabotage the economy, destroy the revolution and thus ensure the continued exploitation and oppression of our people.' In short, 'The IMF and its masters have never invested in revolutions. They only seek to destroy revolutions. Ghana has no right to expect a softer treatment from these imperialist organizations if we are determined to make a true Revolution.'

Here was the key to the political opposition to the IMF and World Bank loans: they would be used to undermine the socialist revolution by the IMF's local allies who were alleged to be on the right-wing of the revolution. Power followed money, therefore the pro-imperialist economic technicians would depose the Marxists.

The JFM had difficulty in understanding how the Secretary for Finance—'a self acclaimed Marxist'—could want to negotiate a deal with the IMF. The IMF's failure to grant a loan to Michael Manley's leftist government in Jamaica was cited as an important cause of his electoral defeat. The outside observer might note an inconsistency in this argument however: if an IMF loan could save Manley's government, it might also save the revolution in Ghana, although other interpretations could be drawn, which are beyond the scope of this work.

In the same editorial, the JFM raised the main economic argument against accepting the IMF loans: the IMF would insist on a package of policies that would affect both workers and farmers. The principal measure would be a massive devaluation of the Cedi which would undermine the standard of living of workers by raising the cost of imported consumer goods. Thus, workers would have to pay more for fewer imports.

Subsequent events have shed some light on the debate as to whether the IMF loans would build or destroy socialism in Ghana. The PNDC devalued the currency from 2.75 Cedis to the US dollar at the beginning of 1982, to 50 Cedis to the dollar by the end of 1984, a devaluation of over 1,000 per cent. By 1984 the open market price of a large tube of Macleans toothpaste in Accra had increased to 250 cedis. The entire monthly salary of the average worker would now be consumed by the purchase of three or four tubes of toothpaste. The Secretary of Finance conceded that another two or three years would elapse before the workers saw a substantial improvement in their standard of living. However, the cause of this delay was not the IMF loans but the long-term effects of mismanaged capital which predated the December 31st revolution (interview, Accra, 8 August 1984).

But by August 1984 Ghana under the PNDC had received loans

worth US$250.4 million in standby facilities, plus US$126.5 million in Compensatory Financing Facilities from the IMF, and US$40 million from the World Bank for economic reconstruction, especially the transportation infrastructure necessary for exports (interview with Dr K. Botchwey, Accra, 8 August 1984; PNDC, *Two Years*, 1984, p. 26). By mid-1984, some reconstruction as a result of the loans was visible: roads and railways were being repaired and rebuilt, the necessary spare parts imported to maintain the vehicles transporting Ghanaian primary products to the ports were more widely available than they had been in 1982 or 1983 before the loans came on-stream. The *New York Times* mainly attributed the 'impressive growth rate of 5 per cent with inflation trimmed from 115 to 140 per cent' in 1984 to the revolution's economic programme, including the IMF loans (May, 24 November 1984). Exports were to provide the necessary funds to pay off foreign loans and to purchase the much-needed goods that would eventually allow a return to the standard of living of the early 1970s with improvements on that.

The IMF loans and the PNDC's encouragement of 'patriotic' Ghanaian businessmen and 'honest' foreign investors are seen by the JFM as not only a retreat from socialism, but a surrender to capitalism. The NDM and the Secretary for Finance, however, have argued that these policies were modelled on Lenin's New Economic Policy (NEP) of the 1920s, which was supposed to build the economic basis for socialism by encouraging capitalists to reconstruct, under socialist control, carefully selected sectors of the Soviet economy shattered by the First World War, its civil war and foreign invasions (interview with Dr K. Botchwey, Accra, 8 August 1984; Carr, 1952, Vol. 2, pp. 269–357). This would appear to be thoroughly Marxist-Leninist, compatible with Lenin's notions of NEP and the process of achieving socialism and Mao's concept of the national democratic phase of the socialist revolution.

Lenin recognized that a revolution passed through different phases and that politically each phase has its own character and tasks, although there are bound to be some overlaps. In April 1918, shortly after the October revolution, Lenin outlined his understanding of a new revolutionary government's political strategy (Lenin, 'Immediate Tasks . . .', 28 April 1918). At the start of the revolution, both before and after the seizure of power from the old regime, 'the first task of every party of the future is to convince the majority of the people that its programme and tactics are correct' (Lenin, 28 April 1918, p. 649). Because of the particular circumstances in Ghana, i.e. threats to the leaders' safety, the December 31st revolution was initiated before a party drawing in all Marxist–Leninists could be formed, let alone a party which had convinced a majority, or even a significant minority, of the Ghanaian people.

On the other hand, the June 4th 1979 insurrection and the subsequent formation of the NDM and JFM, combined with the work carried on by the AYC and the KNRG, had had a considerable impact in spreading socialist ideas beyond the initial, isolated core groups. The net effect, however, has not proved to be the equivalent of a Leninist party with its own political base.

This lack of a political base has given added impetus to the revolutionary leadership to implement a Maoist 'new democratic' strategy of a broad-based alliance of anti-imperialist elements drawn from a number of classes but focused around a Marxist core. At first, this grouping mainly consisted of the NDM and the JFM, then, following the coup attempts of October/November 1982, mainly of the NDM with fragments of the JFM. Other groups such as the AYC, the PRLG and the KNRG were also present, with the AYC increasing its participation after 1982.

Moreover, the 1984 addition of Justice Annan to the PNDC, and the prominence that was given to his role in the PNDC clearly marked an attempt to muster support from the professional and business classes in Ghana. These people had previously been alienated from the PNDC for a variety of reasons. Perhaps the most notable of these were: their anger at the PNDC's attacks on them for the failure of some to pay taxes, the participation of others in corruption, and their resentment at the property confiscations carried out by the revolution. Also significant was the fact that the professionals had had a long history of involvement in constitutional politics. Their anger at the overthrow of the Third Republic, then, was partly altruistic and partly economic in origin.

The inclusion of Mrs S. Alhassan, an 'old' Nkrumahist referred to earlier, in the PNDC in 1984 was intended again to indicate a broadening of the 'new democratic' alliance beyond the categories of

Figure 1 PNDC Ghana (1984): Political Structure

⟹ PNDC political control
⟶ Civil Service administrative control

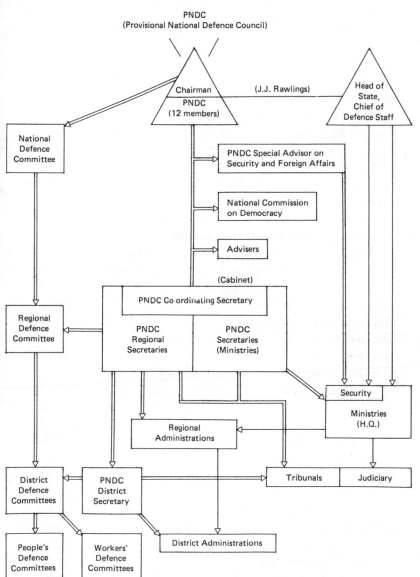

Marxists, security forces, trade unions, intellectuals, civil servants and a variety of 'new' Nkrumahists and other types of anti-imperialists and nationalists. These categories are not necessarily mutually exclusive in Ghana.

Lenin stated that 'the second task that confronted our Party was to capture political power and to suppress the resistance of the exploiters'. The December 31st revolutionaries found it easier to capture power than to secure that power against economic resistance by the business classes (i.e. 'suppress the resistance of the exploiters') or to accomplish Lenin's third task—organizing the administration of the country (Lenin, 28 April 1918, p. 649). The latter reflected on the one hand the lack of support enjoyed by the Limann government, and on the other (i.e. the consolidation of power) the fact that, more importantly, the leaders had made a revolution without the support of a broad-based, trained Leninist party.

The creation of anti-corruption tribunals, the freezing of assets, the confiscation of property, i.e. the 'suppression of exploiters' were fairly easy to implement once the small number of revolutionaries had seized key elements in the state enforcement apparatus. However, limited numbers meant that the revolution was unable to police the markets to enforce price controls (a mechanism which implied benefiting the workers and peasants at the expense of business people). Both the NDM and the JFM realized the necessity of forming a party, but were unable to do so because of lack of time, experience and opportunity and because of differences over strategy and leadership.

The key to the formation of the new party was to be the defence committee system (interviews, Accra, June–August 1984). The defence committees consisted of two types: People's Defence Committees (PDCs) and Workers' Defence Committees (WDCs). PDCs were organized by the community and WDCs were formed at the workplace, whether it was a part of the Ministry of Agriculture, a school, a factory, or a unit of the Army, Navy, Police or Air Force.

In theory, there was a hierarchy of defence committees that extended from the local unit of the PDC with between forty and a hundred members, up to the National Defence Committee, chaired by the PNDC Chairman (i.e. Rawlings) which operated in a democratic centralist manner. At the lowest level, three to five Unit PDCs composed one Block PDC; three to five of these constituted one Neighbourhood PDC; and three to five of these made up the Area PDC, which was the effective membership level.

Three to five Area PDCs were contained in the Zonal PDC Secretariat which actually organized community projects and monitored prices. Several of these were formed under the District PDC

Figure 2 People's Defence Committees (PDCs) and
Workers' Defence Committees (WDCs), 1983

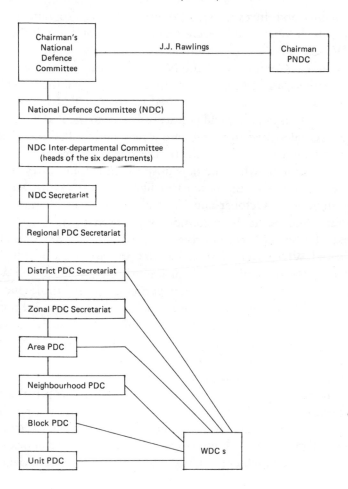

Secretariat which corresponded to the administrative districts and provided the political back-up to the PNDC-appointed political head of the district administration, the District Secretary. The District PDC Secretariats in each region were grouped under their Regional PDC Secretariat, which was the body in charge of the region's political strategy, political education and cadre training.

The National Defence Committee (NDC) Secretariat coordinated the administration of the Regional Secretariats, in particular through the NDC departments: (1) Education and Research; (2) Information and Press; (3) Monitoring and Coordination; (4) Administration; (5) Complaints and Investigation; (6) Projects and Programmes. The NDC, which supervised its secretariat, was the politburo of the PDCs and WDCs; indeed, WDCs were integrated into the above structures. The Standing Committee of the NDC, consisting of a maximum of nine members, was the central executive committee of the structure of PDCs and WDCs. The NDC, chaired by the PNDC Chairman, also acted as a source of policy and political advance to the PNDC. The two bodies were designed to merge into a new body called the National Defence Council, which would be the new supreme revolutionary elected directorate, when the new unspecified revolutionary electoral process merged with the new party-like PDC's structure. Since the coup attempts of October and November 1982 (see Chapter 7), this integrative process has been considerably slowed down.

Like the 'soviets' (committees) of the Bolshevik Revolution, the PDCs and WDCs were designed as the primary units by which the December 31st revolution would promote itself. The PDCs and WDCs were to be instruments of popular participation, political education, channels of communication to and from the leadership, and political control. In short, like the soviets, the defence committees were to be the material out of which a revolutionary party would be formed, but unlike the soviets, the defence committees have come to act as substitutes for a real party organization.

Writing shortly after his return to Russia during the pre-Bolshevik phase of the Russian Revolution, Lenin argued against the revolution establishing a parliamentary republic when a Republic of Soviets of Workers, Agricultural Labourers and Peasants' Deputies could be established from the rapidly emerging system of soviets. The soviets were seen as a proletarian-led alternative to the current Provisional Government which Lenin saw as being controlled by the bourgeoisie, as being reactionary rather than revolutionary. The soviets were perceived to be revolutionary because workers and peasants predominated in their membership, participated in their actions and thus defended their class interests. From their participation in the soviets, Lenin hoped that the workers and peasants would become increasingly class-conscious and better organized, and would increasingly support the aims and activities of the Bolsheviks ('The Tasks of the Proletariat . . .', 7 April 1917, pp. 44–5. See also 'The Dual Power', 9 April 1917, pp. 48–50, both in Vol. 2 of the three-volume edition).

Similarly, Rawlings and the other revolutionary leaders placed great faith in their own equivalent of the soviet—the defence committee. They recognized that, from the start of the revolution the left was fragmented and while revolutionary organizations existed they were not yet a unified revolutionary party with a significant number of members across the country. Soon after seizing power, Rawlings called for the creation of PDCs and WDCs. The initial goal was to create an organizational presence for the revolution across the country. The PDCs and WDCs were thus to act as organizational structures capable of attracting and organizing popular support for the revolution and its goals. The long-term goal was to use the defence committees as the building blocks of the future revolutionary party (interviews, June–August 1984). However, the ideas of using the defence committees as future party cells and as the basis for a future 'people's assembly' were stalled during the latter part of 1982. Some of the most senior defence committee organizers became involved in the attempts of October/November 1982 to replace Rawlings. The coup attempts discredited them in the eyes of the loyalist leadership and a certain guilt by association consequently tainted the concept of the defence committee. The anticipated upgrading of the PDCs and WDCs consequently did not occur.

In December 1984 the defence committees were renamed and restructured, as 'CDRs'—Committees for the Defence of the Revolution—a title used in Burkina Faso and Cuba. The name change reflected the PNDCs desire to include all patriots and to emphasize the national democratic phase of the revolution. The National Defence Committee was disbanded. Instead, the CDRs of each region were made responsible to the PNDC Regional Secretary. A training school for CDR cadres was to be established to upgrade their political skills.

The defence committees were formed after Rawlings' radio appeal for their establishment. The spontaneity of their inception contributed to the uneven quality of the membership and leadership of the defence committees, however. On the one hand, the defence committees have drawn into the decision-making process large numbers of people who, lacking the previous qualifications of wealth, advanced age and high social status (e.g. university graduates and chiefs), had not been able to participate effectively in the running of their lives and their communities.

Figure 3 Committees for the Defence of the Revolution (CDR's), 1985

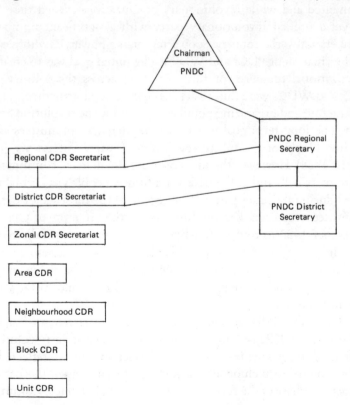

These people had often been excluded from the pre-revolutionary power structures. Those wealthy enough to fund the political parties were able to dominate the former electoral system, and hence the government. The chiefs formed the parallel, though decaying, system of authority to parliament, though they comprised a small minority of the population. In both chieftaincy and party politics, the elders had kept a stranglehold on the decision-making process: even men in their thirties might be called 'small boys'—a serious insult in Ghana. The defence committees broke this stranglehold and acted as a demo-cratizing force in this regard. In the rural areas, a number of bitter battles have been fought between the defence committees and the chiefs.

On the other hand, some leaders of defence committees abused their positions in order to obtain illegal access to scarce resources such as gasoline, cooking oil, etc. These corrupt practices have had the effect of tarnishing the image of the PDCs and WDCs in the eyes of many. Certainly, the top leadership of the defence committees have had to devote a considerable amount of time to rooting out those in the defence committees who had taken the opportunity to enrich them-selves.

Considerable efforts have been made to reorganize and upgrade the quality of the defence committee cadre at the district and zonal level by the theoretically sophisticated and (now) more experienced leaders at regional and national levels. Senior-level leaders are responsible for the political education of middle-level (district and zonal) leaders, who in turn pass it down to the junior levels.

This political education is disseminated through conferences and seminars, lectures, public speeches, government media such as the *Daily Graphic* and Ghana Broadcasting radio and television. In addi-tion, the NDC had its own newspaper, *Nsamankow*, and issued a series of pamphlets. Topics covered range from imperialism to democratic centralism, to Cuba as an alternative model of society, from which to learn though not to be blindly copied. Six-week cadres schools were run in mid-1983. Militia training for PDC and WDC cadres was initiated after the coup attempt of 19 June 1983 and some PDC and WDC cadres have been armed for the duration of anti-smuggling operations. After the first two years of their existence, PDCs and

WDCs were numbered in the thousands and were even present in many villages.

All these efforts at reorganization and training have been hampered by the scarcity of material resources. These have ranged from a lack of writing paper in the Daboya (Northern Region) Zonal Secretariat with which to conduct its business, to the lack of transport for the Damongo (Northern Region) District Secretariat and a lack of cement for the Nima Zonal Secretariat (Accra) to reconstruct the area's housing. There is still a politically crippling lack of experienced, educated cadres. Knowledge of the rest of the world and of other revolutions is limited and acts as a constraint on the cadres, limiting their awareness of lessons that have already been learnt and of other policy options available.

These constraints, plus the confusion generated by the events of October and November 1982, perhaps explain why the revolutionary leadership gave less emphasis after 1982 to actualizing and formalizing the PDCs and WDCs into units of popular government. Instead, more emphasis has been placed on developing the leadership experience of the previously inexperienced cadres through the mechanisms of community development projects. Where this occurs, their credibility with the local people will be enhanced.

Beside the usual activities of leading political discussions and acting as a communications channel between the people and the PNDC, the PDCs have been put in charge of administering community projects. Those projects have included operating the local People's Shop (which sells subsidized goods such as food and soap), some road maintenance and some community sanitation. For example, the Nima PDC in Accra has played an outstanding part in mobilizing the community to restore sanitation in the area. In Limann's time, the stench from the heaped garbage and excrement in Nima even penetrated into passing cars which had their windows tightly shut. Thirty-foot high piles of garbage and excrement have since been removed from the roadside. Trees, flowers and food crops have been planted in their place. Ten community latrines have had their buildings and cesspits cleaned out, and since then they have been maintained by the PDC. The quality and effectiveness of the PDCs and WDCs of course varies greatly across the country.

The PNDC extends what partisan political control it can through the mechanism of the PDCs and WDCs. The PNDC attempts to exercise administrative control over the civil service through the agency of a Cabinet composed of ministerial and regional secretaries, who are the equivalent of ministers, provincial premiers and state governors, to use British, Canadian and American analogies. The Chairman of the cabinet is the PNDC Coordinating Secretary, who is responsible to the PNDC. Since significant numbers of senior civil servants have not been sympathetic to the revolution, the strategic necessity for creating a full party structure capable of supervising the civil service and development programmes as the precondition for building socialism has emerged.

6 Mass Organizations

Nationalist and national liberation movements throughout Africa have historically been weak in material resources, be they transportation, weapons or money. Consequently, they have had to rely on other resources to accomplish their goals of transformation (Saul and Arrighi, 1973; Pratt, 1976; Mondlane, 1969; Hodgkin, 1957; Davidson, 1974). One convenient resource close at hand has been people—who can be organized into mass organizations. Types of mass organization relevant to our argument have taken forms such as ancillary organizations to the party (Duverger, 1964), mass parties (Pratt, 1976; Duverger, 1964) and mass organizations as the first step to the formation of a Marxist–Leninist vanguard party as well as an instrument with which to govern and mobilize political support in the absence of such a party.

Duverger, citing examples drawn from various communist parties, defines 'ancillary organizations' as structures which focus the attention of the masses onto the party by bringing together hitherto relatively isloated supporters or by strengthening feelings of belonging, of membership among the masses, to the party. Ancillary organizations can also be used to gain allegiance by individuals who may agree with only one aspect of the party (e.g. nationalism), to the party itself. The party then hopes to broaden the scope of agreement to the extent that the member of a mass organization can be recruited to the party. Moreover, communist parties, as well as others, have mass ancillary organizations not only as a source of supporters and members, but as a holding-ground for those deemed not quite worthy of full party membership, and also as a means of 'retaining lukewarm members as well as a means of strengthening the loyalty of the faithful'. This can be done through a variety of mass organizations, whether or not they are formally controlled by the party. The functional range of these organizations is immense, ranging from leisure groups (e.g. sports clubs) to single-issue groups (e.g. peace), to demographic groups (e.g. women, youth) to occupational groups (e.g. trade unions, peasant unions). The major object of these mass organizations is to create satellite organizations composed of supporters, directed by party members (Duverger, 1964, pp. 17, 106–7, 118). Duverger assumes the prior existence of a party. In revolutions, such as that in El Salvador, that have had a strategic socialist content, the building of 'popular organizations' went hand-in-hand with building mass support for the revolution and the party, as well as being a prelude to armed struggle (North, 1982).

The term 'mass party' has been the cause of some confusion of definition, but some useful points can be extracted from this very variety. Mass parties (Duverger, 1964, pp. 62–71), in contrast to parties of notables, are dependent on raising the resources necessary to win power by recruiting a large number of members who contribute what in individual terms is rather small compared to the sums derived from the wealthy notables, but which when taken *en masse* adds up, ideally, to a considerable amount. The mass party is thus concerned to expand and keep its membership by giving its members a real sense of democratic control. The party of notables has a very loose membership structure. While it may recruit members from the masses, the notables are primarily concerned with 'how to use the political and financial strength of the masses as an ancillary force' (Duverger, 1964, p. 66): form should not be confused with content.

While these ideal types were developed from European examples, they are applicable to a considerable extent in Africa. After the primary phase of African resistance to European imperialism was over, by the end of the First World War (1918), Africans were faced with the dilemma of how to respond to the continuing European occupation. Should they collaborate, adapt, or resist? In order to make the variety of decisions that Africans did in effect make, they first needed to get a 'road map' of who their occupiers were, what they wanted, and to what they would respond. In short, Africans, once they had recovered from the initial shock of conquest, had to come to some understanding of where the centre of colonial power lay.

The history of the response by Africans to colonial rule displays a wide variety of tactics and strategies. Africans turned to religions, especially Christianity and Islam, as ways of reclaiming some spiritual and emotional freedom. (Gandhi's tactics failed in South Africa just after the turn of the century and again, in the 1950s.) Increasingly, Africans were influenced by a growing understanding of what was happening in their imperial heartlands in Europe, as well as in the United States. After 1917, the success of the Bolshevik Revolution provided another model. The various models were transferred to Africa where they were transformed, to varying degrees, by local organizations and approaches to the problems. African notables were sent by others of their number to negotiate with the colonial authorities. The 'party of notables' model was adopted by what became some of the nationalist movements. Other nationalist movements and national liberation movements were influenced by contact with the 'mass party' model.[1] European communists, socialists and social democrats with their mass parties became the organizational, if not always the ideological, model for Third World nationalists.

The debate among many nationalist leaders came to focus on how to adapt the 'mass party' model to the African reality and to what extent this model depended for its success on having a socialist content, as it often had in Europe. Nationalist and national liberation copied much of the organizational style as united fronts and women's and youth ancillary organizations proliferated beside the main movement or party. Tanzania's nationalist movement followed this approach, even to the extent of coopting the grain-threshing groups into the nationalist movement. After independence, President Nyerere tried to convert the nationalist movement into a mass party (Pratt, 1976), but not a vanguard party (Saul, 1979b).

In Ghana, Nkrumah tried to push the CPP to become more than a party of notables with elements of a mass base. Youth, occupational and a number of CPP mass ancillary organizations were set up. However, this attempts to establish socialism foundered on the 'rocks' of the notables, and on Nkrumah's lack of clarity on the means of implementing socialism—among other hotly-debated reasons (Card, 1975). The Communist Party of the Soviet Union (CPSU) evaluated Nkrumah's Ghana as one of the former colonies which had gained its 'political independence', which had pursued an 'independent foreign policy', and had freed itself from 'imperialist enslavement', but which remained in the 'capitalist system of economy' (CPSU, 1963, p. 404). Nkrumah's party, the CPP, was seen as one of Africa's 'national democratic parties' whose goals were 'to eliminate altogether the consequences of colonialism, to establish a national industry based on priority development of the state sector, to secure the progress of agriculture by carrying out land reforms in the interests of the peasantry and by organizing co-operatives' (CPSU, 1963, p. 413). In short, the CPP was seen as a prelude to the establishment of socialism.

Like the national liberation movements, a 'state of national democracy' (such as that in Ghana under Nkrumah) aimed to bring together a broad coalition of forces that were nationalist, anti-imperialist and democratic in character. Such blocs were regarded as being potentially unstable where the unreliable bourgeoisie of the country (i.e. local business people in competition with foreign firms) gained control of the movement. Such regimes were to be aided in their struggle for economic independence by the Soviet bloc because this would weaken imperialism. Lenin had argued that socialists were obliged to aid the 'more revolutionary elements in the bourgeois-democratic movements for national liberation' so as to strike at imperialist oppression (Lenin, 1957, p. 109). However, it was noted that after formal independence there was still a need for a new stage of the national liberation struggle in order to establish the next stage of the Marxist revolution: socialism itself, under the guidance of a Marxist-Leninist party. Cuba was cited as a model of a revolution that had developed beyond its national democratic and anti-imperialist stage, onto the socialist stage (CPSU 1963, pp. 396–428). Both Angola and Mozambique provide African examples of attempts to transform broadly-based, national liberation movements with the goals of nationalism, anti-imperialism and social justice into parties of 'scientific socialism', i.e. vanguard Marxist-Leninist parties.

However, the overthrow of Nkrumah prevented whatever possibility there had been of turning the CPP into a vanguard party. The left only began to re-emerge with any vigor in the wake of Rawlings' June 4th 1979 uprising. Even then, there was no proper revolutionary party, but a series of movements which, by the start of the December 31st revolution, had only begun to establish links with the masses and with mass organizations such as the trade unions.

If the CPSU had forecast the future of the revolution on the basis of the development of the left, it would have predicted grim prospects. According to the CPSU, there are three main stages of growth that revolutionary communist parties experience in their transformation into 'real vanguards'. Initially, the group is small, isolated and concerned mainly with training their cadre, developing their analysis of their own country as well as with their unity. In the second stage, the group merges with the masses through such political action as strikes and other 'mass actions of the working class'. The party becomes a class-conscious movement working for socialism. Only in the third stage did the CPSU expect the party to become a political force capable of winning the support of a majority of the working class as well as 'considerable masses of the people', i.e. that the revolutionary party would be strong enough to gain power. Moreover, this would only be possible if the party wove itself into the masses and mass organizations such as trade unions, women's and youth associations and co-operatives, in order to mobilize and recruit the masses. The contesting of elections also provided another avenue for contact with the masses (CPSU, 1963, pp. 333–43). The integration of the party into the masses and mass organization was the benchmark for an effective revolutionary party; without it Lenin in 1920 dismissed any party as useless: 'If the minority is unable to lead the masses, to link up closely with them, then it is not a party and is of no value whatever, no matter whether it calls itself a party' (Lenin, 1962, p. 332).

Yet, by 31 December 1981, revolutionary organizations were seizing power barely two years after being formed. They had completed the last task of the CPSU's third stage, i.e. gaining power, when they were only just emerging from the first stage. For example, the New Democratic Movement was still very much in the first stage— organizing itself. The June Fourth Movement had begun the second stage by establishing links with some workers and some junior military ranks. The rules of the 1979 election had prevented revolutionary left parties from using the elections to win mass support: indeed, most of the revolutionary left organizations were founded after the elections had been held. Thus, according to the expectations of Lenin and the CPSU, the 31st December revolution would have been judged to be premature. Perhaps their advice might have been that one of the first tasks of Ghanaian revolutionaries should be to build mass organizations as well as links with the masses. In this way the left would have some means of compensating for their lack of material resources (having seized state power, the left had to control it as well as the wealthy who had controlled and staffed its upper echelons). The building of mass organizations would provide a medium for the masses to participate in the political decision-making that affected parts of their day-to-day lives. Mass organizations would provide the vehicle for politically educating and so upgrading the revolutionary quality of local leaders. Moreover, the building of mass organizations would provide the basis for a future Marxist–Leninist vanguard party. The June Fourth Movement and the New Democratic Movement were aware of these shortcomings of the left and accordingly acted to build mass organizations for the stated reasons above (interviews, June–August 1983 and May–August 1984). The key mass organizations were to be the people's defence committees (PDCs) and the workers' defence committees (WDCs), later reorganized and renamed Committees for the Defence of the Revolution (CDRs).

Defence Committees as Mass Organizations

The overall structure, history and goals of the defence committees as part of the revolutionary governing structure have been analysed in a previous chapter. A brief review only is in order here. The defence committees were brought into being at the start of the revolution for eight main reasons. First, they were to be mass organizations that would allow local-level political participation. Second, they were to be agents of local development, taking part in neighbourhood health and economic projects. Third, the defence committees were to be local agents of revolutionary control: hence they were to act as the information trip-wire against attempted coups, and were even to act as a local militia in defence of the revolution, as some did after the 19 June 1983 coup attempt. Fourth, they were to act as channels of political communication. The defence committees were supposed to pass information up the line, ultimately to the PNDC, and to pass government orders, programmes, etc. and revolutionary education to their members and their neighbours. Fifth, they were supposed to democratize the goods distribution system by operating their own system, which

included People's Shops, which would thus bypass the discredited old
state system of the Ghana National Trading Corporation stores and the
outrageously expensive 'illegal' private traders. Sixth, the defence
committees were intended to mobilize popular support. Seventh, they
were supposed to recruit and train the most talented from the masses,
turning them into a new source of revolutionary leadership. Following
on from these goals, the eighth goal was to turn the defence committees into the nuclei of a new revolutionary vanguard party.

To what extent were these ambitious goals achieved? Defence committees, as mass organizations, in a number of places across Ghana are
now examined in order to evaluate them. The hinterland of a country
has often proved to be a difficult place in which to organize a revolution that originated in the capital. In the case of Ghana, the lack of an
already existing revolutionary network across the country meant that
the December 31st revolution started with only a few pockets of
support outside Accra. Accordingly, the PNDC decided to create
defence committees as the mechanism to extend the revolution into
each village, even if that village or town had had little or no previous
involvement with revolutionary organizations, such as the June Fourth
Movement or New Democratic Movement, prior to 31 December
1981. The defence committees in Daboya, Northern Region, faced
such a task.

Daboya is located some thirty miles west of Tamale, the regional
capital, just below where the White Volta bends to the east, towards its
source. Daboya is a town of perhaps one thousand people sited on
the west bank of the river.[2] Its inhabitants are only connected to the
regional capital and its market by canoes and by a now washed-out dry
season drift. Economically and politically, Daboya has been isolated
from Ghana's mainstream since the imposition of British colonialism
and commerce destroyed the economic base of the Gonja aristocracy
and the old trade routes that passed through Daboya.

Daboya is the capital of the Wasipe province of the Gonja kingdom,
founded in the 1500s. Consequently, there is a layer of political
authority here that predates the contemporary Ghanaian state and with
which any new Ghanaian government must deal. The Gonja aristocracy have dominated the indigenous Hanga and Tampulima peoples of
the Daboya area, as well as incomers to the area and the descendants of

those who were enslaved in pre-colonial times. In pre-colonial times, the aristocracy lived off the slave and salt trades, slaves who worked Gonja farms, and tribute from the indigenous people who farmed. When the British and global markets smashed the slave base of the economy, the aristocracy became impoverished and were unable to support such prestige goods as horses, the symbol of domination by the aristocracy's light cavalry (Case, 1979).

Today, small-scale farming—usually done with a hoe—and fishing dominate the economic life of Daboya. Locally produced foods are traded for other goods in neighbouring and regional markets. The aristocracy competes with market forces for a share of the peasant farmers' time and produce by demanding tribute. These demands contribute to the tension between the aristocracy and the farmers. This was the situation in Daboya into which the December 31st revolution introduced defence committees.

The first defence committees in Daboya were organized in February 1982. The PDC was dominated by the literate youth: students, junior civil servants such as teachers, nurses and sanitation workers. Significantly, they tried to invite illiterates such as peasants and fishermen to join, in order to broaden their political base and conform more closely to the democratic mass ideals of the revolution, but few in fact joined. The chiefs were excluded, though it is doubtful whether they would have wanted to join an organization founded by young people which challenged the traditional undemocratic power structure. The first Daboya PDC was like so many other PDCs at the time: it lacked the clear goals and supervision that could be translated beyond mere words into a local reality. A member of the Daboya PDC later stated: 'We didn't know what to do' (interview, Daboya, 29 July 1983). This PDC eventually became inactive.

On 4 November 1982, a second-generation PDC was organized. Successful efforts were made to broaden the membership's demographic profile. Numbers of illiterates joined the PDC, indeed, one became its chairman. Sons of the Wasipewura, the Chief, joined the PDC, and one became its secretary and effective leader. Although the PDC membership included the range of ethnic groups in Daboya from Gonja to Ewe to Akan-speakers, the executive was once more dominated by Gonja.

The Workers' Defence Committee represented civil servants in Daboya and although it was independent in matters such as the working conditions of government employees, the PDC was supreme in matters concerning other aspects of life. While the functions of the WDC only affected the affairs of the civil servants in Daboya, the PDC operated within and outside Daboya. The Daboya PDC was active in community mobilization and decision-making. It assisted the people of the nearby villages in organizing their Defence Committees. The Daboya PDC made some attempts to try to educate the other farming villages on the essence of the December 31st revolution. They were hampered, among other things, by their lack of a clear understanding of what those goals were and of how to implement them.

The Daboya PDC was also involved in the distribution of scarce goods. Goods distributed by the PDC came from central government supplies, such as consumer supplies—rice, tinned milk, soap and batteries—as well as agricultural necessities such as fertilizers. The benefits of this distribution system to the nation and the people of Daboya were supposed to be several. First, by reducing the influence of private middlemen who were instrumental in inflating prices, it would facilitate the decline in inflation. PDC-distributed items were to be sold at the government-designated price, which in most cases was one-tenth to one-third cheaper than that of the 'free-market' or hoarded price. Goods brought to Daboya by the PDC were sold through the various representatives of the town's sections and civil servants, thus ensuring that each town section, and in most cases each family, would receive some share of what was distributed. This method of distribution was also designed to ensure that goods that were meant for the community at large were not amassed by a privileged minority. The PDC tried to fix prices for products such as locally-produced food whose supply was not controlled by the government. The setting of prices for such goods to some extent followed the 'free-market' prices of the traders and farmers.

Information from the PNDC, NDC, or RDC (Regional Defence Committee) in Tamale and decisions taken by the PDC were communicated to the people through their clan representatives and also by the local town crier. The PDC in turn was supposed to inform the central government about the decisions and suggestions of the people of Daboya. These efforts at intercommunication, articulation and aggregation met with limited success. On the key issues of building a bridge across the White Volta, discussed below, the PDC was unable to mobilize local political support to any significant extent, nor was it able to get impounded Daboya funds or other aid to construct the bridge.

Another major concern of the Daboya PDC was the economic and social development of the town. The PDC was involved in the supervision and maintenance of government installations. As part of the PDC's development programme, the PDC mobilized communal labour to dig pit latrines as well as to repair the road and the bridge to Damongo (the district capital). In the latter case the PDC transported an electric generator to the government clinic in Daboya, but was unable to get it installed.

The PDC's most significant economic development project was its attempt to build a bridge across the White Volta. This bridge would be capable of carrying heavy traffic such as trucks and buses, and would open up the Daboya area and its hinterland to Ghanaian (and world) market forces and new ideas, unimpeded by the traditional power structure which had controlled the ferry. The bridge would have replaced the canoe ferry which carried people, goods and livestock and the washed-out concrete drift (which had only been of use during the dry season).

The immensity of the task can be seen from a comparison between the sum raised in Daboya during 1980 and the 1984 construction estimate. As a result of a fundraising campaign led by the pre-PNDC Daboya Town Development Committee, and sanctioned by the Wasipewura, some 14,000 Cedis were raised. The Daboya PDC estimated the cost of the bridge linking the Daboya area to the regional capital at 3.6 million Cedis (*Ghanaian Times*, 30 December 1983).

While the Daboya PDC had some success in broadening the democratic basis of decision-making by establishing a new structure— the PDC—which brought young people and non-Gonja into the political realm, the PDC had trouble changing the habits and traditions of the people. Among other things, this was due to the fact that a large proportion of the PDC membership were part of what kept the traditional system alive. Both kinship and economic relationships were the main linchpins between the PDC and the traditional system. Since most members of the PDC were not economically independent and since the PDC operations were voluntary, most of the Daboya PDC executives were dependent, in one way or another, on their relatives. Many of these cherished the traditional system because they had benefited, or else hoped to benefit, from the power structure. It was often difficult for the PDC, therefore, to be firm on issues concerning the traditional system from which many of the first- and second-generation PDC executive members stood to benefit. Thus, the Wasipewura and the 'River Sub-Chief' in charge of the ferry were never directly confronted over their extraction of tribute from local people and what some believed to be their behind-the-scenes opposition to the building of the bridge (the bridge would have further undermined part of the source of revenue of the traditional system).

The Daboya PDC established itself as a link, varying in effectiveness, between the people of Daboya and the central government. It became an institution that tried to win over the people of Daboya to the aims of the PNDC, and to help them feel part of the decision-making process of the country. The PDC symbolized the goals of the December 31st revolution in Daboya. The PDC was most successful in its tasks of political communication, symbolism and mobilization. The PDC achieved much less in the functions of development project implementation and in establishing itself as the dominant political authority. Nevertheless, the threat which this organ of local revolutionary power came to represent can be measured by the fact that, in 1984, the Chief's family, having lost its considerable influence in the third-generation PDC—renamed the Daboya PDC Zonal Secretariat—proceeded to attack the PDC over the issue of the bridge.

The bridge over the White Volta represented an economic and political threat to the traditional power structure in Daboya. Inhabitants of Daboya were entitled to a free canoe ride across the White Volta, but non-Daboyans and every item of goods was subject to a tax or tribute payable to the River Sub-Chief. Thus, the Sub-Chief derived a considerable part of his income from his control over the canoe ferry. A portion of this revenue was passed on to the Chief, the Wasipewura. A bridge or government-operated ferry would obviously disrupt this source of income for the Gonja nobility, and alternatives would be more difficult to control, partly because the traffic could not be controlled.

As the Chief's family lost control of the PDC, so the lower nobility and the peasant youth elements gained in influence. These new PDC leaders entered into an alliance with the Town Development Committee, which was then controlled by a group of older, non-royal proto-business men. The young people sought to demonstrate their ability and their commitment to improving Daboya and its hinterland. The proto-business men wanted to use their new wealth, generated by their participation in local markets, to increase their social status and open up new business opportunities. Both groups stood to benefit from the building of a bridge or government ferry, but the Gonja office-holders stood to lose.

The pro-bridge alliance of the PDC and the Town Development Committee decided that the only way to build the bridge or ferry was to raise money from the people of Daboya and the surrounding villages. This could only be done by sending messengers to the villages to explain what was to be done, who would benefit and how much people should contribute. This in turn could only be done by messengers on petrol-powered mopeds and motorcycles. However, since petrol was very scarce, one of the proto-businessmen volunteered to find the petrol and donate the cost of it if the Daboya PDC and the District Defence Committee would obtain official authorization for his purchase.

When the barrel of petrol finally arrived in Daboya, it was stored in the businessman's house. The Chief's sons then accused the PDC and the Town Development Committee of stealing the petrol and planning to sell it illegally. The Ghana police detachment in Daboya were induced by the Chief's sons to 'arrest the barrel of petrol' in early 1984. The net effect was a block on the bridge fund campaign, as well as an attack on the reputation of the PDC and the Town Development Committee (interviews, Daboya, July 1984).

The PDC retained some influence and continued to act as an alternative revolutionary (if somewhat unsteady) route for upward political mobility that in effect challenged the traditional political structure and its attendant economic base. However, the lack of support from the Regional Defence Committee for the Daboya PDC had meant that the

PDC as a mass organization was increasingly in danger of collapsing at some future time under pressure from the traditional power structure. Such an outcome would negate the possibility of the PDCs forming the cells of a future party.

Other Examples of Defence Committees

The Nima Area PDC of Accra has been examined in a previous chapter. A third example of how PDCs operate as mass orgnizations has been chosen from a regional capital. The District Defence Committee Secretariat for the Western Dagomba District had its headquarters at Tamale, the Northern Region capital, where it received more supervision and resources from the Regional Secretary and the regional coordinator of defence committees than had been available to the remote Daboya PDC Zone. For PDC purposes, in 1984, the district was divided into twelve zones, each zone being subdivided into five areas, each of which was further subdivided into units. The secretariats of each level, down to the zone, were paid by the government. Each level's secretariat was appointed by the next highest level.

At each level there were supposed to be five committees: Political Information and Research Committee or Bureau, Monitoring and Coordinating of PDCs and WDCs Committee, Projects and Programmes Committee, Investigation and Complaints Committee and Administration. The degree to which these actually existed at each level varied greatly across the country. A brief word on the ideal functioning of each district-level committee is in order to see how these basic units were intended to function on a day-to-day basis.

The Political Information and Research Bureau issued press releases, organized rallies and 'study cells', and researched local problems. Intermittently, it had taken part, with the National Youth Organizing Commission, in efforts at mass education, notably a literacy campaign. The Bureau tried to raise the political awareness of the cadres at each level within the district by organizing them into 'study cells'. Topics covered included Lenin's definition of class, primitive communism (called, in this case, the communal system), slavery and the other stages of economic development, 'rules of the December 31st revolution' racism, apartheid in South Africa, Zionism in Israel, and principles of Marxist–Leninist organization such as democratic centralism and how to put them into practice.

Monitoring and Coordination oversaw the working of lower-level PDCs and WDCs, including the election of executives and the solving of internal PDC and WDC problems.

The Projects and Programmes Department were to draw up and implement development projects based on locally-voiced needs. For the Tamale area, these ranged from running community farms to rebuilding clinics and obtaining drugs for other aspects of the Primary Health Care programme, to setting up and operating People's Shops. The previously-mentioned Nima Area PDC in Accra had transformed Nima into a showcase of PDC-led development projects with the resurrection of their sanitation system and the operation of a food factory.

Investigation and Complaints dealt with dissidents. It had ten broad 'matters of concern':

1. economic stability, i.e. preventing traders from selling goods above the control price; 2. preventing the embezzlement of government funds; 3. preventing smuggling; 4. preventing hoarding—the prelude to

Figure 4 District Defence Committee Secretariat

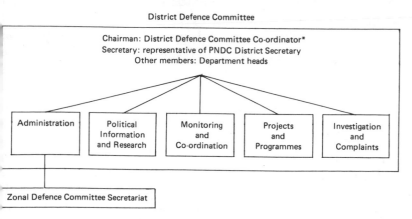

District Defence Committee

Chairman: District Defence Committee Co-ordinator*
Secretary: representative of PNDC District Secretary
Other members: Department heads

| Administration | Political Information and Research | Monitoring and Co-ordination | Projects and Programmes | Investigation and Complaints |

Zonal Defence Committee Secretariat

* District Organizing Assistant after 1984

selling above control price; 5. preventing stealing; 6. preventing the falsification of state funds, e.g. over-invoicing; 7. preventing the misuse of government property, e.g. the private use of public vehicles and machinery; 8. preventing illegal foreign currency trading; this was more of a problem in Accra than in Tamale where only one case had been identified up to August 1984; 9. preventing the diversion of fuel to illegal sales; and 10. preventing 'subversion', which was more of a problem in the border areas, which attempted coup-makers would invade on their way to Accra, than in Tamale.

Cases were dealt with on a class basis: more leniency would be shown to a worker or peasant than a senior civil servant.

Administration was in charge of the initial review of all problems as they came to the notice of the District Secrtariat, and consequently allocated the problem to one of the other committees. It also dealt with outsiders on behalf of the Secretariat, routine administration and the disposal of supplies sent by the Regional and National Secretariats.

Evaluation of Defence Committees as Mass Organizations

The problems for the Daboya defence committees were symptomatic of problems experienced by many defence committees across Ghana. The creators of the defence committees underestimated the strength and resilience of the traditional power structure. This underestimation reflected the youth, newness and, up to this date, mainly urban experience of the Marxist and populist creators of the defence committees. In Accra, it is possible to discount the traditional rulers since they are overwhelmed locally by the panoply and might of the Ghanaian state, and by the processes of urbanization and integration into the global economy. Away from Accra, a king was able to publicly taunt members of a District Defence Committee Secretariat, knowing that he had more of a political base locally than they had and that the withering away of the Ghanaian state during the 1970s and early 1980s hindered their ability to call upon it for help in the absence of a well-organized revolutionary party. In short, while the defence committee structure had begun to analyse the traditional power relationships, the grassroots leaders of the PDCs and WDCs found themselves on occasion thrust into situations of not understanding the local power dynamics—where the threats would come from and how to overcome them.

Not only did the leaders of these mass organizations often lack the tools of analysis, they often lacked a knowledge of organizing skills that come with experience or from a well-organized, well-staffed supervising structure. Here, the inexperience of the leaders of the defence committees from the National Defence Committee downwards told against them.

The last socialist regime, and one of a rather superficial and immature type, had been overthrown on 24 February 1966. Apart from the populist interlude of 4 June to 24 September 1979 of the AFRC, Ghana's socialists and radical populists had not had the opportunity of exercising state power since 1966—over fifteen years before the start of the 31 December 1981 revolution. Thus, as of 31 December 1981, the revolutionaries could count one, possibly two, experiences of state power. The AFRC period lasted less than four months, the Nkrumah socialist period was ended over fifteen years before the PNDC assumed power. The more experienced leaders such as Captain Kojo Tsikata had participated in and been inspired by a vision of socialism generated by Nkrumah's socialist youth movement, the Young Pioneers, which was modelled on their namesake in the Soviet Union (interview with Captain Tsikata, Accra, 1 August 1984). Rawlings was eighteen years old at the time of Nkrumah's overthrow. Many of the original revolutionary leaders would have been children and in their teens when this happened.

The overthrow of Nkrumah and the harassment of the Nkrumah-ists and other sections of the left under a variety of subsequent governments disorganized and partly paralysed them for many years. Not until 1979, under the AFRC and then the Third Republic, was it possible to set up overtly Marxist organizations: before that there had been a number of study groups, etc. The Marxist organizations, founded in 1979 and 1980, had a brief experience of building support (only two and a half years) before they took part in the seizure of power, the running of the state, mobilizing support for the revolution and themselves, and fighting off counter-revolution. Based on their largely theoretical and conspiratorial experiences, the revolutionary leaders lacked practical aptitude for implementing their strategies when they seized power.

The defence committees were reorganized several times. However, each reorganization carried with it some confusion in the minds of the members as to what the defence committees were supposed to do, who should be a member, who the leaders were, how they were supposed to be chosen and what their duties were. Moreover, these disruptions were compounded by sectarian argument between the left organizations and the attempted coup by part of the June Fourth Movement and the consequent PNDC purge of them.

A series of pamphlets and the newspaper *Nsamankow* were established by the INCC (later the NDC) to clarify these points, and they also developed the political acumen and organizing skills of the defence committee members (interviews with NDC members). However, their circulation was mainly limited to the national, regional and district capitals, as well as other major cities in the south. How many people who received this literature actually read it, and of those how many understood the articles and knew how to apply them to their everyday work is a matter for conjecture.

Yet, despite all the problems associated with the defence committees as mass organizations,[3] and the inability of the PNDC to turn them into the constituent units of a new revolutionary party, the defence committees have made remarkable contributions to the revolutionary process. The defence committees did provide a vehicle for popular participation. They were set up right across the country, allowing some elements of the revolutionary process to penetrate into remote areas and they did broaden the base of the revolution by recruiting a variety of elements. Indeed, they were a source of political mobility. They also acted as channels of political communication, variable in quality though these might be. As mass organizations, they proved to be effective in passing political intelligence to the PNDC security forces, thus helping to prevent or destroy attempted coups. A few defence committees received military training and did attempt to physically defend the revolution against armed opposition, as in the case of the 19 June 1983 attempted coup, or against economic attack, as in the case of helping to patrol the borders against smugglers. They did take part in a number of development projects, and formed the basis for attempting to establish a more equitable system of goods distribution. So, for all their problems, the defence committees were invaluable to the revolution since they created a political breathing space for the PNDC and helped to pin down or disrupt the opposition.[4]

Youth and Women's Mass Organizations

Defence committees have been the most significant mass organizations of revolutionary youth and women in terms of their participation, office-holding and as structures existing on a national basis. Yet their participation and ability to win election or appointments to the highest offices has been tempered by the larger society's under-valuation of women and youth, as well as by factors such as class and education. Again, it should be noted that in Ghana 'youth' can apply to those in their thirties, or even forties, as opposed to the teens and early twenties of North America and Europe. In Ghana, the older youth, usually male, were able to play a significant part in the defence committees, while the younger revolutionary youth, both male and female, have found themselves taking part in organizations specifically devoted to youth, such as the Student Task Force, the National Youth Organizing Commission (NYOC) and the Democratic Youth League of Ghana. If defence committees form the body politics of mass organizations, then, by comparison, the revolutionary youth-specific organizations are but skeletal, and revolutionary women's organizations are mere embryos.

In 1982, the central thrust of the revolution's youth policy was to 'inject into the youth, the spirit of patriotic nationalism and the feeling of oneness and Pan-Africanism, with a view to creating for them a national and continental identity' (PNDC, *Guidelines*, 1982, pp. 34–5). Accordingly, the revolutionary leadership wanted to build mass-membership youth organizations that would implement these political values as well as development projects. These projects, together with political education provided by revolutionary cadres, were seen as being instrumental in accomplishing the ideological goal. Young people were to be organized to contribute to the political and economic sides of the revolution.

Once more, the revolutionary leadership faced the ever-present problem of the shortage of cadres, of creating revolutionary mass youth organizations where none had existed before. There were a variety of youth organizations which predated the revolution and a number of these, such as the Muslim Youth Association, the Ghana United Nations Students and Youth Association, various secondary school students, the African Youth Command and the post-secondary National Union of Students, came out in support of the revolution (*Ghanaian Times*, 6 January; 3, 4, 6 February; 6 March 1982). These did not owe their primary political allegiance to the revolution, however. Instead, the PNDC established the National Youth Organizing Commission and the Student Task Force.

The Student Task Force, announced by Rawlings on 5 January 1982, was launched within two weeks of the beginning of the revolution as part of its vanguard (*Ghanaian Times*, 11 January 1982). The Task Force membership was drawn from students at the three universities (Legon-Accra, Kumasi and Cape Coast), from other post-secondary institutions and secondary schools. It was first set up in the university towns and was initially focused on what became the successful movement of 100,000 tonnes of Ghana's main export, cocoa, from the rural areas, as well as on community projects (*West Africa*, 19 April 1982). The Greater Accra Student Task Force repaired roads, began removing the rubbish accumulated during the previous regime, bagged fertilizer to help get agriculture going and assisted in community health projects (*Ghanaian Times*, 16 January and 3 February 1982). In non-cocoa growing areas, such as Daboya in the Northern Region, the local Task Force was composed of the secondary school students and graduates who had been active in the Daboya Student's Union. They were unsuccessful in getting non-students to initiate self-help projects in Daboya, although the Task Force had more success in other parts of the country. The Task Forces had some success in controlling the price of goods in the markets (*Ghanaian Times*, 2 March 1982; interviews, Accra, Daboya, 1983, 1984). They also helped organize defence committees.

Once the students had accomplished much of the immediate task of transporting the cocoa to the ports for export and food into the cities, by early April their initial patriotic fervour had begun to wane. While there had been attempts by the left wing to conduct political education among the rest of the students who comprised the majority, most of these had in fact been motivated by a temporary wave of patriotism that had overcome their usual mode of class behaviour. The majority had very limited perceptions of what constituted a revolution. Even where the political education by the left was conducted skilfully, linking local situations to larger realities by non-rhetorical theory, there was very little time for it to be put into practice. Students began to voice the desire to return to their studies in order not to interrupt their university year.

Voting at the zonal, district and regional levels of the Task Force showed the division over whether to end or to extend this body. The Ashanti Region demonstrated a pattern of opposition to the left-wing revolutionaries that was part of the regional pattern. Students in fifty-one of the eighty-six zones voted to return to their studies. In what was then the Upper Region—a stronghold of the June Fourth Movement—the key districts of Bolgatanga (the regional capital), Navrongo and Sandema voted for an extension. Despite the statement of the National Union of Ghanaian Students that the district Task Forces had voted 49 to 33 for a six-month extension for the Task Force, it began in fact to be closed down, and was eventually replaced by other bodies. Most of the students returned to their universities and schools on 23 April 1982 (*Ghanaian Times*, 6, 13 April 1982 and *West Africa*, 3 May 1982). Some elements of the Task Force remained until September, as in Daboya, but they were eventually either absorbed into defence committees and other agencies or else they fell by the wayside.

The student leadership's evaluation was that the Task Force had been effective in an emergency situation and that it had received support from local people (Libya, and Ghanaians themselves had provided food). However, there had been logistical problems, caused by the suddenness of its creation and there was a need for reorganization (*Ghanaian Times*, 13 April 1982). The Task Force demonstrated some of the strengths and weaknesses of spontaneity in the implementation of mass organizations. The Task Force was successful as the single blow that cut Ghana's Gordian knot of an apparently hopelessly blocked transportation system that was obstructing the export of Ghana's economic life-blood—cocoa. But like Alexander's original swordstroke, the Task Force was unable to solve the underlying root of the economic problem. Only a continuing mass organization could have contributed to the long-term solution. Here the inexperience of the youth leaders told against them in organizing the students and raising the revolutionary consciousness of what were essentially elitist students whose medium-term interests dictated a return to their studies. Nevertheless, the Task Force did help to prepare the way for other more enduring mass organizations such as the defence committees and the National Youth Organizing Commission.

In early February 1982, the PNDC Secretary for Youth and Sports, Z. Yeebo, announced that the pre-revolutionary National Youth Council was to be reconstructed into a mass revolutionary youth organization. He criticized the old National Youth Council as a vehicle of bourgeois counter-revolution. Following Nkrumah's overthrow, the National Youth Council had been set up by the United Nations to replace Nkrumah's socialist and radical youth movement, the Young Pioneers, which had been modelled on its namesake in the Soviet Union. The Secretary cited with approval the example of the youth movement of the Democratic People's Republic of Korea which had played a key role in transforming the economy of North Korea. This stood in stark contrast to the failure of the capitalist interregnum (1966–81) governments to mobilize youth. The December 31st revolution saw revolutionary youth as the bedrock of national emancipation, for the fight against imperialism and colonialism. Accordingly, a new youth movement was to be established, in which young people would receive ideological training to promote nationalism, patriotism and discipline. Primary and middle schools were to be mobilized into brigades which would produce cadres for the national youth movements (*Ghanaian Times*, 8 February 1982).

Early in the third month of the revolution, steps were taken to implement these goals. The Ministry of Youth and Sports created a fifteen-member committee to draw up the draft of a national youth movement which would focus its efforts, like that of the Student Task Force, on economic and community development, including the fight against illiteracy, disease and hunger. The National Youth Organizing Commission began to gather resources, train cadres—often former secondary and post-secondary students now fulfilling their compulsory period of National Service—and establish projects across the country, starting with the national and regional capitals (*Ghanaian Times*, 4 March; 12 April 1982).

As part of this process, the National Youth Organizing Commission organized the Democratic Youth League of Ghana for children between the ages of 6 and 14. In many ways, the League (formed on 19 November 1982 in Accra) was an extension of the Commission, but was designed for a younger age group. Kwasi Adu was Chairman of both the Commission and the League. At other levels, there was an overlap in the leadership. The goals of the two organizations were similar, with the League giving more emphasis to sports and to teaching applied skills to the children to help them contribute to Ghana's economic development. Healthy, productive, patriotic, anti-imperialists were the hoped-for result. Both organizations were based on Nkrumah's Young Pioneer movement (WA, 29 November 1982, p. 3112).

One of the National Youth Organizing Commission's successes was the formation of the Tamale Youth Home in Tamale, the Northern Regional capital. The building and grounds were expropriated from the Gymkhana Club, formerly frequented by senior civil servants. The District Coordinator and fourteen other members of the National Youth Organizing Commission organized the children into two groups of the Democratic Youth League of Ghana, with forty-three children in the 6 to 12 age group, and one hundred and nine in the 13 to 21 group. Two-thirds of the children were male. Initially, the Commission members, nearly all of whom had been teachers, recruited members for the League by going into the Tamale schools in mid-1982 to talk about the League. Many joined in this early enthusiasm for the revolution.

The Commission members, who are paid, organized programmes of sport, patriotic songs and short talks and discussions on the political economy of Ghana and the world. For example, the children demonstrated an awareness of the problems of peace and racism in southern Africa. League members were divided into groups named after African liberation leaders, such as Steve Biko House (i.e. South Africa), Kwame Nkrumah House (Ghana), Amilcar Cabral House (Guinea-Bissau) and Patrice Lumumba House (Congo/Zaïre). There was little equipment, but there were a number of wall posters from Cuba, El Salvador,

Ghana's revolution and the World Assembly for Peace (interviews with Commission and League members, 27 June 1984; personal observation June–August 1984). While the numbers of young people involved in the project were small, the quality of political education was impressive. The political potential of those involved indicated that the programme seemed to be succeeding in terms of the quality if not numbers recruited and the development of future revolutionary cadres.

The need for women's revolutionary organizations was recognized early in the revolution. In March 1982, the June Fourth Movement called on women to form a mass national democratic movement to fight the oppression which had reduced them to second-class citizens. Addressing themselves to the significance of International Women's Day (March 8) for Ghanaian women, the June Fourth Movement exhorted women to change their ideas. Women could increase production, just as men did, in order to rebuild Ghana. Women should stop thinking of themselves as inferior since this hindered the achievement of revolutionary democracy. While there was thus a tendency to blame women for allegedly contributing to their own subordination, the June Fourth Movement had at least recognized that women were discriminated against at a personal as well as a structural level. For example, it was argued that men in positions of revolutionary authority should stop harassing market women because the women were not the cause of the capitalist impoverishment of Ghana's economy but a symptom only. The market women sold at above control prices but it was the multinational corporations which dominated the economy and stole Ghana's natural resources (*Ghanaian Times*, 9 March 1982).

The next move came on 17 May 1982. The December 31st Women's Movement was formally inaugurated at Burma Camp, Accra. (The membership included the wives of armed forces personnel.) The aims of the club were to conduct political education among women by focusing on the goals of the revolution, as well as helping them to form economic ventures which would increase their financial self-sufficiency. Rawlings attacked the stereotype of women as 'evil', cheating market women when he argued that the economic and political conditions of capitalism had forced women into 'kalabule' in order to be able to feed, clothe and educate their children.

Nana Agyeman Rawlings, Jerry Rawlings' wife, was one of the leaders of the December 31st Women's Movement. All the original six branches were founded in the Greater Accra area (*Ghanaian Times*, 17 May 1982; *West Africa*, 31 May 1982, p. 1484), and the movement had great difficulty expanding beyond the national capital. For example, as early as November 1982, women in the Upper West Region were complaining that they had often been excluded from the different revolutionary organs, yet they made no reference to the December 31st Women's Movement (*Daily Graphic*, 7 November 1984). In mid-1984, PNDC member Mrs Aanaa Enin organized the formation of the All Women's Association of Ghana (AWAG) in Accra. This is a group of organizations which aims to coordinate the concerns of women's organizations generally.

Summary

The revolutionary youth mass organizations had a much smaller membership and coverage of the country than did the defence committees. The former were outnumbered by youth movements not affiliated to the revolution. The Student Task Force was the most effective of the revolutionary youth movements in terms of economic development. The revolutionary youth mass organizations suffered from a shortage of experienced revolutionary leaders. The revolution's need for cadres to control the state drained away many potential leaders. The attempted coup of October/November 1982 led a number of youth leaders, including the Chairman of the National Youth Organizing Commission and the Democratic Youth League of Ghana, to resign and leave the revolution. The problem of building an anti-imperialist youth mass organization in the national democratic phase of the revolution in the absence of an overt socialist party was never effectively confronted. Nevertheless, the youth organizations played their part in promoting the acceptance of egalitarian and revolutionary ideals.

Hampered by lack of experience, the absence of a revolutionary party, a shortage of resources, lack of a tradition of revolutionary women's organizations, and the transfer of many women leaders to run the government, the revolutionary women's movement was a mere embryo mass organization compared to the defence committees. The December 31st Women's Movement remained small, drawing its membership mainly from the wives of armed forces personnel in the Accra area. However, the fact of its creation signified an awareness on the part of the revolutionary leadership, some of whom were women, of the need to deal with the problem of women and of the need to draw them into the revolution if it was to succeed in its long-term goal of liberating Ghanaian society generally. At the same time, it should be noted that women were members of other mass organizations such as the youth groups and the defence committees. The influence of women in these organizations was limited but it was there.

The revolution's greatest success in creating mass organizations was the establishment of defence committees. Despite their problems, they allowed the revolutionary leadership to come into contact with large numbers of Ghanaians across the whole country. The PNDC was only able to achieve something like a monopoly for its mass organizations with the defence committees as organs of local government. But even here, they were sometimes challenged by the traditional authorities. The defence committees as mass organizations provided a forum for political participation for the lower classes in Ghana. Politically naive, sometimes very disorganized, they nevertheless gave room for manœuvre to the PNDC.

Table 3 Membership of mass organizations

Mass organization	Membership*
Defence Committees	500,000
Student Task Force	6,000
National Youth Organizing Commission	800
Democratic Youth League of Ghana	7,000
December 31st Women's Movement	1,000
All Women's Association of Ghana	20,000

* Note: overlapping membership occurs

7   Political Dissent from the PNDC

Political dissent from the PNDC has taken a variety of economic and political forms. Economic opposition has included the smuggling of goods and currency, the selling of goods inside Ghana at prices above those set by the government, the misallocation of resources controlled by the civil service and the state corporations, together with other measures designed to sabotage the economic policies of the PNDC. Political opposition to the PNDC ran the gamut from resignations from the revolution, to a hostile editorial policy, to criticism from the hierarchy of some churches, to organizing political movements such as the Campaign for Democracy in Ghana, to attempts to overthrow the PNDC by force.

Economic Opposition

Politically-motivated economic opposition should be distinguished from ordinary economic crimes. The distinction is necessary for two reasons. First, it reveals the class warfare that underlies the economic reality of Ghana. Second, the economic criminal and the practitioner of certain traditional customs cannot be equated with those who opposed the government on purely partisan grounds: the two former categories would not be recognized by foreign governments as eligible for political asylum.

Economic crimes may be distinguished from economic opposition on the basis of intention, although in practice the former may be subsumed by the latter on the basis of the effect of what is actually done. Economic crime is motivated by greed. Economic opposition is designed to sabotage the government's effectiveness, and thus further weaken the government's political base. Its instigators may be disgruntled individuals, as was the case with a number of prominent Ghanaian business men, business women and civil servants, acting either in isolation or in a class network of contacts. Such economic opposition may be linked to opposition groups operating abroad.

These in turn may be linked to foreign governments intent on promoting a counter-revolution. Economic sabotage has formed an integral part of the strategies used by governments hostile to socialist or socialist-orientated revolutions: Britain, France and Germany used their own as well as Russian agents against the Bolsheviks (Carr, 1952, vol. 2). Many Portuguese settlers wrecked much of the transport and machinery in Mozambique when they left at Mozambique's independence in 1975. The American CIA were involved in the publication of a booklet for the 'Contras' that detailed how to create economic chaos in Nicaragua.

Finally, economic habit can be identified as the third category of economic opposition. In situations of extreme economic crisis, people may engage in activities such as smuggling and buying and selling on the black market, which in effect constitute economic opposition to the government and which fall also into the realm of economic crime. However, these small-scale activities can be distinguished from the other two categories in that they are motivated by the individuals's fight for survival. For example, many civil servants buy their allocation of tinned milk and other goods at the government-controlled price and then immediately resell them at a much higher price on the black market in order to make the extra money necessary to buy enough of the cheaper, basic local foods to feed their families through the month. This practice, which is technically illegal and in effect undermines the revolutionary ethic, is a function of survival. While it was strongly opposed during the early stages of the revolution, by 1984 there was a *de facto*, if unwilling, tolerance of it. This was based on a growing perception by the revolutionaries that until the revolution's economic strategy had resulted in goods flooding the market, ordinary people would be forced to supplement their incomes in this way. Again, this points up the revolutionaries' class perception of the different kinds of economic opposition, crime and custom. The first two of these activities were believed by revolutionaries to be dominated by certain senior officers, former politicians, professionals and Ghanaian and foreign business people: in short, the different factions of the bourgeoisie and their supporters. Economic custom was believed to be practiced by the small fry: workers, peasants, junior civil servants and the lower ranks of the armed forces.

As Ghana's economic crisis grew rapidly during the 1970s, it aggravated certain of these tendencies. Elements of Ghana's civil service became demoralized. Despite the fact that a number of Ghanaian administrations from the colonial period onwards had expected the civil service to play some sort of interventionist role in the economy, one study found that Ghanaian civil servants did not see any significant link between the performance of their job and their career prospects. They had little interest in promoting the development of Ghana (Price, 1975). Of course, as the economic chaos grew, it lent a certain logic and legitimacy to the search for extra income by some civil servants. For some of them a pattern of behaviour developed in which they misused the resources available to their office, accepted bribes, or else continued to draw full-time government salaries while engaged in other money-making activities on a part- or full-time basis. For example, government tractors, fertilizers, fuel and labourers were diverted for the private use of public officials (personal observation and interviews, Ghana, 1983–4). The motivation for this since the start of the revolution seems to have been a combination of greed and passive opposition to the government. Other civil service techniques of passive resistance included withholding information and policy alternatives, and diverting and sabotaging socialist initiatives. As another example, a timber merchant complained to Rawlings and the Secretary for Finance that his timber exports were being held up at Takoradi port because the official in charge of signing the necessary export document had not been at his post for six months and his deputy had not been seen for a month (personal observation, Osu, 7 August 1984).

How effective has this unholy alliance of economic opposition, crime and custom been in weakening the revolution? Precise figures are of course not available, but some sort of estimate is possible. During the short-lived June 4th 1979 revolution, eight generals (including three former heads of government) were shot for corruption. This action indicates that among junior ranks of the armed forces these generals were held personally responsible for the suffering of workers, peasants and junior ranks and their families caused by the economic crisis. Corruption on this scale was seen as a blood debt, repayable only by the firing squad or by long prison sentences

(Oquaye 1980, pp. 138–45; interview with PNDC member, Justice Annan, Accra, 4 August 1984).

Significantly, two days before the executions took place, the AFRC set up military Special Courts to try corruption cases (Amnesty International, July 1983, p. 2). This form of public tribunal was used to regularize and bring under control the by-passing of the 'regular' courts which had proved so ineffective in dealing with corruption. These new AFRC public tribunals tried many of the officer corps, civil servants and the wealthy for corruption. One hundred and fifty-five of these were given prison sentences that ranged from six months to ninety-five years! Just before the handover to Limann's civilian Third Republic, the AFRC announced that a further sixty-eight people who had fled the country had been sentenced for corruption. Despite attempts to enforce these prison sentences by adding 'Transitional Provisions' to the new Constitution, some sentences were overturned during the Limann period. In contrast to the severity of the AFRC measures against corruption, Limann's new anti-corruption tribunal only imprisoned some five people, and dropped AFRC charges against a further sixteen (Amnesty International, July 1983, p. 2). Clearly, the AFRC under Rawlings established a stern precedent for dealing with economic corruption and crime. This carried over into the period of the December 31st revolution.

When Rawlings took power for the second time, he declared that the revolution was to be a 'holy war' against the corrupt (Rawlings, 31 December 1981). Anti-corruption measures were announced, as there were signs that corruption continued and even infected the lower ranks of the revolution in the defence committees. Special courts, called Public Tribunals, were set up to deal with economic obstruction and crime, as well as attempted coups and plots. The Public Tribunals, announced in January 1982 (*West Africa*, 18 January 1982, p. 197), only came into operation some seven months after the revolution had begun. Once again, these tribunals should be seen as an attempt to impose order on an anarchic situation in which, lacking a well-organized revolutionary core, all kinds of revolutionary justice had been meted out with very little central control. The Public Tribunals were created as an institutional way of dealing with attempted coups and other security problems as well as economic opposition and crime

The extent of the economic opposition and undermining of the revolution's aims can be measured in part by the number of cases and types of sentences handed down. Over one thousand cases were brought before the tribunals in their first year of operation (PNDC, *Two Years*, 1984, p. 17). Sentences ranged from imprisonment to execution. For example, in November 1983, one tribunal sentenced to death two people *in absentia* who had been convicted of stealing rice from Ashanti Region farms. In another case a corporal was sentenced to death for murder (Amnesty International, 'Death Penalty Log', November 1983, p. 1). A conviction for stealing from the Ghana Commercial Bank by an employee resulted in a death sentence (Amnesty Interantional, 'Death Penalty Log', August 1984, p. 1). The first death penalty for smuggling was handed down by a tribunal in early October 1983, the execution being carried out in September 1984 (Amnesty International, 'Death Penalty Log', October 1983, p. 1; September 1984, p. 1). Besides those found guilty of economic opposition and crime, the tribunals also sentenced to death many soldiers and others who took part in attempted coups.

Plots and Attempted Coups

Political opposition to the PNDC and the December 31st revolution has also been expressed through plots and attempted *coups d'état*. Rumour has often been rife in Accra with reports of who attempted what and who was shot at dawn: a disruption in the electricity supply was often sufficient to trigger a rumour. Up to the middle of 1986, the most important coup attempts were the events of October/November 1982 and of 19 June 1983. These attempts, together with a selection of other recorded attempts and plots, provide significant insights into political opposition in Ghana under the PNDC. Given the paucity of concrete analysis of this most important form of political opposition to the PNDC, some reconstruction of the nine coup plots and attempts,[1] and of personnel involved is necessary for an understanding of emerging patterns.

Coup Plot: 'Operation Sadat', March 1982

Barely three months after the start of the revolution, security forces discovered an attempt to copy the assassination of President Sadat of Egypt. Rawlings was to be murdered in this 'Operation Sadat'. Some twenty-one people including Captain Owoo (a former Military Intelligence officer and participant in the AFRC) were reported to have been arrested on suspicion of taking part in the plot (Amnesty International, July 1983, p. 12).

Coup Plot: Discovered July 1982

In July 1982 revolutionary security forces broke up attempts to overthrow the PNDC by killing some of its members. While some of the suspected plotters fled, six junior officers and ranks were arrested, including Flying Officer Ebenezer Odoi (a former prosecutor of the AFRC Special Courts 1979). When arrested, he held a senior position at PNDC headquarters (Amnesty International, July 1983, p. 12).

Amnesty International states that it first heard of the arrests on 25 July 1982. The timing of the arrests suggests possible connections either with the emerging disagreement within the revolutionary forces or with the murder of the judges on the evening of 30 June 1982 by a number of people who had links with the revolution (see Chapter 4). One of those arrested, Corporal Amedeka, was later tried and executed for this murder.

Attempted Coup: 29 October 1982

On 29 October 1982, at a meeting of the Accra and Tema WDCs, some of the leaders of the June Fourth movement and the People's Revolutionary League of Ghana announced that Sergeant Akata-Pore, a leader of the JFM, Secretary of the Armed Forces Defence Committees and an original member of the PNDC, had replaced Rawlings as Chairman of the PNDC. Apart from this announcement, the protagonists took no other step: this attempt must rank as being the only example of coup by press conference.

Confusion reigned in Accra until Rawlings was notified, where-upon he declared that he had not been replaced. On 12 November, in an attempt to glue back together the revolutionary coalition, Rawlings called a press conference. Seating the principal instigators of the coup behind him, Rawlings stated to the media that there had been a misunderstanding but that it had been resolved. This figures as one of the more magnanimous ways of resolving an attempted coup.

However, when another group attempted a coup less than two weeks later, on 23 November, PNDC security forces rounded up the group as well as Sergeant Akata-Pore and 'some 40 of his military supporters' (AI Index AFR, 28 August 1984). Chris Atim, another PNDC member and JFM leader, resigned from the PNDC and went into exile in Britain, from where he has since made verbal attacks on the PNDC government. Others connected with the October attempt also resigned from the revolution and left Ghana. Another member of the PNDC, though apparently with no connection with the October event, Brigadier Nunoo-Mensah, also resigned on 23 November.

The events of 29 October 1982 crystallized certain divisions within the revolutionaries' forces. The JFM leadership (which in reality came to exclude Rawlings, particularly after 31 December 1981) and the People's Revolutionary League of Ghana had hoped to move quickly on the open establishment of socialism. However, Rawlings and other revolutionaries believed or came to believe that this was not possible. By May 1982, the JFM called for an open declaration of full socialism rather than Rawlings' commitment to the national democratic phase of the revolution.

The tension was increased by the question of foreign assistance. Chris Atim, PNDC member and a JFM leader, canvassed the Soviet Union, Czechoslovakia, the German Democratic Republic, Bulgaria, Hungary and Cuba during March 1982 in search of massive funding to rehabilitate the Ghanaian economy. As some PNDC leaders began to realize the enormous scale of the funds at low interest rates that were needed and compared these to the obviously inadequate Ghanaian and Eastern bloc sources, they turned to the IMF and the World Bank (interview with Dr K. Botchwey, Secretary for Finance, Accra, 8 August 1984).

The key political question faced by the revolution in this respect was: would the IMF, the World Bank and the capitalist countries only trade aid for the betrayal of the revolution? Rawlings, Botchwey, the New Democratic Movement and the technocrats answered no; the JFM and the PRLG answered yes. By August, the JFM believed that the PNDC had begun negotiations with the IMF. By September, these negotiations were publicly acknowledged by the PNDC. At the end of October, JFM and PRLG leaders tried to depose Rawlings and establish a more purely socialist regime.

Chris Atim explained his reasons for resigning from the PNDC in a bitter letter (Atim, 3 December 1982). Writing after the events of 23 November 1982, Atim accused Rawlings of having been responsible for the derailment and betrayal of the revolution in his search for personal power. Atim accused Rawlings of threatening both himself and Sergeant Akata-Pore at the PNDC meeting of 27 October 1982 (two days previous to the JFM attempt) when they would not agree with him. Atim maintained that the attempted coup of 23 November was in fact organized by Rawlings as one of his 'attempts to frame us up'. The JFM, led by Atim and Akata-Pore, was portrayed as having been overcome by Rawlings, the NDM and other alleged forces of counter-revolution. Both sides traded accusations of tribalism, with Rawlings and the Ewes supposedly on one side, and Akata-Pore and the Northerners supposedly on the other. (See also the resignation letter of Kwasi Adu, JFM President, dated 31 December 1982, as well as W.A., 29 November 1982, p. 3066, and 6 December 1982, p. 3133–4).

Attempted Coup: 23 November 1982

The second, most nearly successful attempted coup was that of 23 November 1982. The analysis of this attempted coup is complicated by two separate chains of events, already mentioned, one of which was rooted in the October attempt, the political effects of which were still being played out over two years later.

The 23 November attempt actually went as far as armed conflict small arms and mortars were used for an hour. Part of Gondar Barracks in Burma Camp, Accra was captured for a short time by the instigators of the coup (*West Africa*, 29 November 1982, pp. 3065–6). By the next day, apart from the imposition of a longer curfew, the search for the instigators, a general round-up of certain opposition suspects, and pro-government rallies, life returned to normal in Accra.

The initial list of nine soldiers suspected of the attempted coup included two majors, three lieutenants, one warrant-officer and three lance-corporals (*West Africa*, 6 December 1982, p. 3133). Twenty-six of the suspects named later were armed forces personnel. These included one captain, four warrant-officers, ten corporals and six rankers (Amnesty International, July 1983, p. 13; Amnesty International Index AFR, 28 April 1983; March 1983; *West Africa*, 8 August 1983, p. 1852), as well as one policeman and two civilians. They were brought before a Public Tribunal in Accra on 15 March. Thirteen were tried *in absentia*, the rest in person. The trial was interrupted on 19 June 1983 when a number of the defendants escaped as part of that day's attempted coup. After a lengthy trial, Kwame Pianim, the economist, received an eighteen-year prison sentence, and the others were either acquitted or escaped (Amnesty International Index AFR, 28 July 1982, 4 October 1983).

Besides those arrested on suspicion of having taken part in the 23 November attempt, those believed to have been connected with the 29 October events were also arrested. Some twenty people, mainly left-wing members of the National Defence Council and its Secretariat who were associated with the JFM and the PRLG were arrested during 24–30 November, including Tata Ofusu, editor of the JFM's paper, *The Workers' Banner* (Amnesty International, July 1983, p. 13). On 30 November, the PNDC announced that a number of left-wing soldiers, including Sergeant Akata-Pore of the PNDC and JFM, had been arrested on charges of mutiny (Amnesty International, July 1983, pp. 12–13; *West Africa*, 6 December 1982, p. 3133).

To add to the confusion of this period, with two coup attempts within a month and the subsequent arrests of both left and right, as well as rumours that the 23 November attempt was connected with the American embassy and Victor Owusu (a right-wing leader), on 22 November 1982 (*West Africa*, 29 November 1982, p. 3065), Brigadier Joseph Nunoo-Mensah (PNDC member and Chief of Defence Staff) handed in his letter of resignation, dated 23 November.

After stating his support for 'a fundamental political and social change which would ensure a reasonable measure of economic prosperity for the broad mass of our [i.e. Ghanaian] people', Nunoo-Mensah went on to explain why he was resigning. He claimed that the cost of the revolution was too high (a charge that is not well argued or substantiated in his letter). More importantly, he claimed that more discipline was needed within the armed forces, defence committees, on the street and at the work-place. Even more significantly, he argued that the political process was stalling, as evidenced by the PNDC's failure to go ahead with an 'Armed Forces convention' and the botched implementation of the defence committee concept, as well as by the bypassing of certain PNDC members, as evidenced by the secret landing of weapons without his (Nunoo-Mensah's) knowledge.

Also, on 23 November 1982, PNDC member J. Amartey Kwei confessed to having taken part in the murder of three judges and a retired army officer (the so-called 'judges murder') during the night of 30 June-1 July 1982. The events of October/November 1982 were a period of great tension and confusion for the revolution as serious opposition from both within and without became manifest.

Coup Plot: Discovered 27 February 1983

Security forces broke up a suspected coup plot on 27 February 1983. At least nine soldiers were arrested, two of whom were later executed without formal trial at the Air Force station, Burma Camp, Accra (PNDC announcement of 2 March 1983, cited in AI, July 1983, pp. 13, 16). One report suggested that the American embassy staff, together with Victor Owusu, a major right-wing party leader who had lost to Limann, were connected in some way with the plot (*AC*, **24**, No. 17, 17 August 1984, p. 7).

Coup Plot: Discovered 16 June 1983

Lieutenant-Colonel Ekow-Dennis, Major Sam Okyere, Captain Edward Adjei Ampofo and ex-Warrant-officer Joseph Okae Kwakye were alleged to have plotted a coup, which was disovered on 16 June

1983. In the confusion surrounding another, and major, attempted coup that occurred three days later, Captain Ampofo and Lieutenant-Colonel Ekow-Dennis eluded punishment. However, together with the other two, they were tried in August 1983 by a Public Tribunal and sentenced to death. Ex-Warrant-Officer Okae Kwakye's sentence was commuted to life imprisonment. Major Okyere was shot on 13 August 1983 (Amnesty International Index: AFR, 28 June 1984; *West Africa*, 22 August 1983, p. 1976).

Attempted Coup: 19 June 1983

The attempted coup of 19 June 1983 came the closest to overthrowing the PNDC of all the attempts and plots discussed in this chapter. Yet, like the events of November 1982, there are certain ambiguities concerning the objectives and motives of those who carried out the 19 June attempted coup.

There was no ambiguity in the fighting itself. Rebel soldiers based in Togo attacked two prisons in Accra and one at Nsawam, outside Accra, in the early morning of 19 June 1983. They freed fifty-two soldiers, most of whom had formerly been in Military Intelligence (who had been responsible for harassing Rawlings and Captain Tsikata during the Limann regime), or had been accused of taking part in the coup plots and attempts of 23 November 1982, 27 February 1983 and 16 June 1983 or in the 'judges murder' of 30 June 1982. Most of the escapees successfully fled to Togo. Other rebel soldiers then moved to capture the studios and broadcasting facilities of the Ghana Broadcasting Corporation (GBC) which they held for over two hours. The rebels made several broadcasts before the PNDC forces were able to contain the attack on GBC. PNDC member Warrant-Officer A. Buadi led his bodyguard against Gate 2 of Broadcasting House while the aptly-named Captain Courage Kwashigah, an Ewe, and his commando dropped from a helicopter onto the roof. After stiff resistance, the twelve rebels were overcome and Kwashigah announced that the PNDC were back in control. (He was promoted to major for his services.) The other rebels tried to escape, some successfully, some were captured and others shot in gunbattles.

The key rebel leaders of the raid were Sergeant Abdul Malik who led the raid on the prisons, and Corporal Carlos Halidu Giwah who announced himself over rebel-held GBC radio as the rebel Operational Commissioner. The political associations of these two are interesting. Malik was the former bodyguard of ex-PNDC Brigadier Nunoo-Mensah (who resigned on 22 or 23 November 1982). Malik had escaped arrest after 23 November by fleeing to Togo. Giwa was reputed to be a former bodyguard of Rawlings (*AC*, **25**, No. 12, 6 June 1984, p. 3) and Sergeant Akata-Pore, the PNDC member with whom he was arrested following the 23 November coup attempt. Giwa was freed by the 19 June raid. Since both Malik and Giwa were executed following their capture after their 23 March raid, one can only speculate as to their alliances. Both were part of the early core of the revolution. Whether or not Giwa and Malik had belonged to the June Fourth Movement which attempted the 29 October 1982 coup is uncertain, but they did cooperate in the coup attempt of 19 June 1983 and in the 23 March 1984 attempt they were caught together as they tried to slip across the border from Togo into Ghana. Precisely where their political allegiances lay by that time is not clear.

The 19 June coup attempt came the closest to overthrowing the PNDC of all the plots and attempts up to mid-1986. The numbers of soldiers involved, the amount of fighting, and the number of government buildings captured were much greater than in the other attempts. Yet the 19 June attempt failed to effect a change of government. It did act as a recruiting device: many soldiers accused of taking part in earlier attempts against the PNDC were freed and made their way to Togo. These gains were partially lost when two key figures of this group, Sergeant Malik and Corporal Giwa, were captured and executed in March 1984. Like all the coup plots and attempts so far, this one was the work of a few people; although there were manifestations of sympathy in Accra, Kumasi and Tamale after the rebel capture of Broadcasting House on 19 June 1983, these were not organized and were not linked to the attempt.

A certain ethno-regionalism may be discerned in this attempt. Many of the participants were northerners. As a result of the attempt, the Sixth Battalion of Infantry, based in Tamale, Northern Region, was effectively disbanded as a combat unit, being reduced to the status of a training unit. A number of those involved in the 19 June attempt had been members of the June Fourth Movement, which had originated among northerners. Finally, many of those soldiers reputed to have been summarily executed after the attempt were northerners (AI Index, AFR, 28/11, 3 July 1984). These soldiers from the north played a significant part in opposing the PNDC, especially after the two most important northerners had lost their influence over the PNDC. However, while northerners played key roles in this particular attempt, most of those who were blamed for it by the PNDC were from the south.

Attempted Coup: 23 March 1984

The attempted coup of 23 March 1984 depended on its initial phase on the successful infiltration from Togo and Ivory Coast of former Ghanaian soldiers who were hostile to the PNDC. Revolutionary security forces, however, broke up this attempt when they captured eleven of the infiltrators and subsequently executed them, on 24 March. Three of these, including Sergeant Abdul Malik and Corporal Carlos Halidu Giwa, had been sentenced by the Public Tribunals for taking part in previous plots (Amnesty International, August, 1984, p. 3).

Coup Plot: 31 January 1985

Another group of northerners sought to assassinate Rawlings in Kumasi during the celebrations commemorating the fiftieth anniversary of the Asante Confederacy's restoration, on 31 January 1985. Their plan was to shoot Rawlings as he gave a speech before the Asantehene (King of the Asante) and a large gathering of Asante. This plot by northerners to assassinate a man with an Ewe mother in the midst of the Asante held the potential for a civil war based on ethno-regional lines.

Rawlings had chosen one of the plotters as his translator. The others, fearing they would shoot their fellow plotter by mistake, did not fire and dispersed after the ceremony. On 2 February, they were discovered at the house of the translator and chief conspirator, Alhaji Abbas Mensah, by security forces. Following a gunfight, during which some of the conspirators escaped, the house was blown up (interview, 1985; *Concord Weekly*, 25 February 1985, p. 5).

Coup Conclusions

These nine coup plots and attempted coups were instigated by junior officers and ranks of the armed forces: civilians played little part in this form of opposition. The major, partial, exception is that of 29 October 1982, in which some civilian members of the defence committees of Tema and Accra and of the June Fourth Movement did take an active part.

Coups have come from both the left and the right, but regionalism has played nearly as important a role as ideology.[2] Northerners have played a leading role in the most important attempts. The 19 June 1983 attempt is significant partly because northerners of different political persuasions took part in it. Nevertheless, southerners, including Ewe, have also taken part.

Prior to the events of October 1982, participants in coups were from the military who were connected with the *ancien régime* but opposition broadened to include sections of the left during the events of October/November 1982. By the 19 June 1983 attempted coup, the opposition was perceived by the PNDC to include not only elements of the military and the left, but also leaders of the student and professional movements as well as top business men and their press. Significantly, these had also been key elements in the successful campaign to overthrow General Acheampong (Oquaye, 1980). The decision by the PNDC to include these non-military elements demonstrates both the seriousness of the 19 June attempted coup as well as the PNDC's worry that the opposition was growing and was within striking distance of overthrowing the PNDC, as it had Acheampong. There has been an increasing tendency for the government to resort to death sentences, executions and summary executions since the 19 June 1983 attempt.

Other Opposition Groups

Other forms of opposition have gathered around Ghanaians abroad, around the Movement on National Affairs (MONAS) and some leaders of the professions and university students. One source of expatriate opposition is from London—Elizabeth Ohene with her magazine, *Talking Drum*. Ohene, former editor of the Accra-based *Daily Graphic*, started her magazine in September 1983. Her constant attacks on the PNDC, among other things, have given her magazine a distribution of less than 5,000 (*AC*, **25**, No. 17, 15 August 1984, p. 8).

The two major movements of the Ghanaian opposition abroad were the Campaign for Democracy in Ghana and the Ghana Democratic Movement. Both were based in London, but had members and sympathizers scattered throughout Western Europe, notably in West Germany and North America. The Campaign had active branches in Lome, Togo and Lagos, Nigeria.

The Campaign for Democracy was founded by Major Boakye-Djan who had a long history of conflict with Rawlings that is traceable to their rivalry in the 1979 Armed Forces Revolutionary Council. Their differences were reputedly a mixture of personal rivalry (Boakye-Djan was number two to Rawlings in the AFRC), power bases (Boakye-Djan was an Akan from the Brong-Ahafo Region and Rawlings was seen by some as being an Ewe from the Volta Region), and political ideology (Boakye-Djan was supposedly to the right of Rawlings). At any rate, disagreements between them contributed to the rapid handover on 24 September 1979 by the AFRC to the incoming elected government of President Limann.

Limann rewarded Boakye-Djan with promotion to major and a scholarship to Britain, which he accepted. Rawlings rejected similar offers from Limann, and was soon forced to retire from the forces. Their separate careers were a point of contention between Boakye-Djan and Rawlings. In 1980 Boakye-Djan attacked Rawlings by calling on the Limann government to investigate certain members of the former AFRC (*AC*, **21**, No. 9, 1980, p. 7).

Boakye-Djan was one of the founders of MONAS, the Movement

on National Affairs. MONAS was active during the Limann regime (1979–81) but was quickly suppressed by Rawlings after his accession to power on 31 December 1981. Following this, Boakye-Djan's opposition to Rawlings was formalized, with the founding of the Campaign for Democracy in Ghana. Boakye-Djan became Co-ordinator but was to some extent eclipsed by J. H. Mensah's Ghana Democratic Movement (see, for example, the Campaign's advertisement opposing the government in *West Africa*, 30 October 1983, p. 2320. See also *AC*, **25**, No. 17, 15 August 1984, p. 8). Another leader of the Campaign was Major Mensah Poku, an Akan from the Ashanti Region who had been active in the AFRC. The Campaign described itself as a new, non-partisan organization, free of any ties to the old parties of the Limann period. Their chief goal was said to be 'the restoration of a human and representative government in Ghana', which meant the restoration of some sort of parliamentary system such as that which existed under Limann's Third Republic (*West Africa*, 3 October 1983, p. 2320). The Campaign was funded by Ghanaian business men abroad.

The Campaign has been accused of having links with the United States government and its Central Intelligence Agency. Captain Kojo Tsikata (retd.), then PNDC Special Adviser on security and now PNDC member, has alleged that a report from the West German embassy in Accra had noted that US Ambassador T. Smith had met on a regular basis in Lome, Togo with Campaign leaders Major Boakye-Djan and Colonel David Zanlerigu, former Limann Minister of Works and Housing. During their discussions of 23 March, 7 April and 10 June 1982, topics covered were believed to have included how to promote tribalism in the military and counter-revolution among the chiefs (*West Africa*, 11 April 1983, p. 872). The PNDC later renounced this statement in the interests of its relations with West Germany (*West Africa*, 6 June 1983, p. 1374). What the PNDC would have said if they had known that one of the leaders of the 19 June 1983 attempt, Corporal Giwa, had signed in at the West German embassy on 23 June is open to speculation.

The main political and financial forces behind the Ghana Democratic movement were those of J. H. Mensah and others of the Popular Front Party of the Third Republic (1979–81) and members of Limann's People's National Party such as Kofi Batsah and Francis Badgie (*AC*,

26, No. 5, 27 February 1985, p. 3; and *West Africa*, 3 October 1983, p. 2320). J. H. Mensah had already had a volatile political career. Finance Minister and cabinet colleague of Victor Owusu in the civilian government of Busia (1969–72) which was overthrown by General Acheampong (1972–8), Mensah in turn was accused in October 1975 of attempting a coup against Acheampong.

While Mensah gained prestige in the London expatriate community after 31 December 1981, both the Ghana Democratic Movement and the Campaign for Democracy lost support from expatriate Ghanaian businessmen. Many of them withdrew their support from the Movement and the Campaign as they contemplated new business opportunities in Ghana. These opportunities had become evident as the PNDC adopted more business-orientated economic policies, in conjunction with the granting of loans from the IMF. At the same time, the London expatriate opposition lost an important leader when Chappie Hutton-Mills died in 1983 (*AC*, **25**, No. 20, 15 August 1984, p. 8; **25**, No. 20, 3 October 1984, p. 6).

The effectivenes of these opposition groups has been minimal in comparison with the attempted coups. Their main significance has been to act as an external irritant to the PNDC by making hostile statements as well as representations to Western governments. Some aid may have been delayed or blocked by them. In a similar manner, within Ghana, opposition from elements of the professional and business classes has been fragmented and of a formalistic nature. The hierarchies of the major Protestant and Roman Catholic churches, as well as the Association of Recognized Professional Bodies and the National Union of Ghanaian Students (which had become conservative by 1983) have all issued statements calling for an end to the December 31st revolution and for the need to re-establish what in effect would be a government in which they played important roles. Their elitist nature however, did not elicit much sympathy for their search for power from Rawlings the populist. The apparent involvement of some professional and student leaders in the 19 June attempted coup and the events of the previous two months led the PNDC to crack down on them—one measure perhaps of their growing effectiveness.

The aftermath of the murder of the three High Court judges and the retired officer on the night of 30 June 1982 was used by professionals and church leaders as a pretext to attack leading members of the revolution (see, for example, the various funeral orations, letters and articles printed in the University of Ghana's *Legon Observer*). These criticisms became muted after the conviction and execution of PNDC member J. Amartey Kwei in August 1983 and the 19 June 1983 attempted coup.

The Movement on National Affairs was perceived by elements within the PNDC as a potential threat, for two apparently contradictory reasons. MONAS was seen as a competitor for the support of socialists within the armed forces and the student movement. Also, MONAS had been founded by one of Rawlings' erstwhile collaborators, Major Boakye-Djan, mentioned earlier. Within days of the start of the revolution, the leaders of MONAS were rounded up. Some of them were detained until early 1984. Among those arrested on suspicion of membership of MONAS were Frederick Blay, a lawyer in Takoradi (arrested February 1982, released 31 December 1982); Yaw Abdu-Larbi (arrested April 1982, released 31 December 1982; Kweku Baako and Kwesi Agbley (arrested 1982, possibly released in 1983) (Amnesty International, July 1983, pp. 13–14).

Before concluding this discussion of the opposition, some mention should be made of the use of samizdat tactics. Within Ghana and amongst Ghanaians abroad, a system of clandestine publication of opposition literature exists. For example, the letters of resignation of PNDC members are copied time and again, retyped or photocopied and are distributed around the country and the world by Ghanaians who travel. One anti-PNDC leaflet circulating in Accra in June 1984 attempted to sow discord by raising such spectres as tribalism and the fear among officers that they would be shot by their own men ('The Watcher Now Being Watched by Ghanaians', 7 pages).

A more transient form of opposition was generated by the rumour-mill of Accra. In one of the more entertaining rumours, the courage of Rawlings was questioned in reports that each night Rawlings and his family slept in a submarine (a yellow one, like that of the Beatles) that was attached to the castle by a tunnel. Despite the fantastic nature of these rumours, the PNDC found it necessary to establish a column in the *Daily Graphic* to refute them.

Conclusions

Between 1981 and mid-1985, political opposition to the PNDC remained fragmented, personalized and ineffective. There is little evidence to suggest that the externally-based political movements have been able to link up with dissidents in the military. Under these circumstances, the PNDC has been able to control the armed forces— the only institutions with weaponry sufficient to offer effective opposition. Economic opposition has often been a matter of personal survival or greed. The circulation of pamphlets is a far cry from overthrowing the PNDC. A group of coup-makers has to succeed only once, of course, to change the regime: the 19 June 1983 attempt came the closest to success.

8 Policies of the PNDC

The foreign and domestic policies of the PNDC amply demonstrate the constraints under which the Ghanaian revolution labours. In the areas of economics, labour, education, culture, women's affairs, military affairs and external relations, the lack of a broad-based political movement at the start of the revolution and the extreme economic problems of Ghana have greatly limited the implementation of the revolution's aims. Yet the revolution has created a certain amount of room for manœuvre.

Economic and Labour Policy

The PNDC's economic policies have ripped apart the Ghanaian left, led to an attempted coup, confused the foreign left into silence if not opposition, aroused the hatred of the domestic business and propertied classes, and have been rewarded in turn by massive loans from the IMF, the World Bank and other bastions of Western capitalism as well as by smaller amounts of economic assistance from the socialist countries.

These economic policies have been used as the litmus test of the revolution's purity by friend and foe alike. Were these policies in fact a version of Lenin's NEP (New Economic Policy) (Carr, Vol. 2, 1952) which promoted a limited, controlled restoration of capitalism in certain sectors in order to kick-start the war-ravaged economy so that production would grow and could then be used to build the economic basis of socialism? Certainly, prominent Marxists in the government have argued that this was really the case. They reasoned that, given Ghana's ravaged economy and the fact that the revolution was in its national democratic phase, the first priority was to restore production, and the only available capital was to be found with the IMF and the World Bank. Liberals in the PNDC also argued for these policies on the grounds of pragmatism and the need to promote production for the benefit of the country. *The Workers' Banner*, the newspaper of the June Fourth Movement, bitterly attacked even the idea of negotiating with the IMF as a betrayal of the socialist revolution. To accept loans from the IMF was seen as being a type of heresy, an IMF heresy. Ghanaian economist James Ahiakpor used the PNDC's IMF loan decision to argue that dependency theory and socialism were unsound (Ahiakpor, 1985). In the face of such divergent interpretations, there is clearly a need to examine what was actually done, why, and to what effect. First, however, it is necessary to give a brief review of the economic policies of previous Ghanaian governments which formed a significant part of the political context into which the PNDC first came to power.

Constitutional independence in 1957 was not matched by a fully integrated economy. Ghana had been engulfed by the world economy, but not totally transformed by it. The export of primary products such as cocoa, gold and timber dominated Ghana's economic activity. If Nkrumah had not chosen the name 'Ghana' to replace the colonial 'Gold Coast', he could just as easily have chosen 'Cocoa Coast' to mark the importance of cocoa in terms of generating the foreign exchange with which much of Ghana's infrastructure was built in the 1950s and 1960s, as well as employment and wealth for Ghanaians and others abroad. Nkrumah encouraged the growth of manufacturing, but this growth, significant as it was, was not sufficient to restructure the economy. The dependence on imported capital equipment and consumer goods, including food, manifested the weak links within the economy. When the world price of cocoa declined, it greatly hindered Nkrumah's industrialization strategy.

Nkrumah had intended to reduce Ghana's dependence on cocoa by industrialization but, ironically, he increased this dependence by using exports to finance the expansion of industry.[1] Incompetent management further hindered Nkrumah's efforts at an economic transformation (Card, 1975; Gore, 1984; Killick, 1983). Moreover, agricultural production, the economic mainstay, was not significantly increased, while increasing sums of money were spent on much-needed services such as education and health. Influenced by W. A. Lewis and others, Nkrumah tried to break out of underdevelopment by using a 'big push' of industrialization to achieve a critical minimum of self-sustaining growth. Central planning was therefore necessary. In turn, Nkrumah's vision of socialism in Ghana focused in practice on the growing control of the economy by the state through state enterprises (Birmingham, Neustadt & Omaboe, 1966; Gore, 1984; Jeffries, 1982, and Killick, 1983; *Wall Street Journal*, 4 January 1982).

By the late 1950s and early 1960s, the economic infrastructure and productive capacity were consuming 80 per cent of planned government investment in search of economic take-off. Using enormous amounts of foreign exchange, Nkrumah established a significant base for Ghana's economy: the Akosombo hydroelectric dam complex (with all the attendant costs of resettling the thousands of displaced people), the Tema port with the industrial base attached, the Black Star shipping line, international airports at Accra and Tamale, roads, bridges, state farms, public housing, health facilities, schools (free for the colonially-deprived northerners) and free universities. By 1965, 53 per cent of all companies were either public or joint public–private operations. Nkrumah's vision was an extraordinary one.[2] Unfortunately, poor management, among other factors (Killick, 1983), condemned much of this vision to poor implementation. The private sector was not of central concern to these policies. Funding was put into private farming co-operatives, but, as in other parts of Africa, for example Zambia (see, e.g., Ray, 1979), they did not succeed. As urbanization pulled people out of agricultural production and as foreign exchange earnings from cocoa declined, Ghana's ability to either produce or buy the necessary food declined.

Nkrumah's search for foreign exchange to finance his policies ran into problems. While he sought to build state control of the economy, the largest pools of foreign capital were controlled by countries unsympathetic to socialism. Nkrumah was accordingly forced to seek the necessary foreign exchange from cocoa exports, and later, also from the use of deficit financing. The foreign exchange reserves were virtually exhausted by the time Nkrumah was overthrown by the NLC junta.

The NLC (1966–9) cut ties with socialist orientated countries and allied itself closely with Western countries. The NLC's attempts at cutting public expenditure and privatizing state corporations were unsuccessful in promoting widespread economic growth.

The Busia regime (1969–72) was also unable to stem the economic tide. In November 1969 Busia expelled many foreigners who had been working in Ghana. As economic conditions deteriorated throughout 1971, Busia came under pressure to repay Ghana's foreign debts, to continue significant expenditure on some social services such as health and education, to subsidize imported urban foods, and eventually to devalue the currency. Three weeks after Busia's government devalued the Cedi by 48.6 per cent, it was overthrown by a military coup (Chazan, 1983).

This military junta lasted in one form or another from 1972 to 1979. General Acheampong controlled first the National Redemption Council (1972-5) and then the Supreme Military Council (1975-8) before he was pushed aside by General Akuffo's Supreme Military Council 'Mark II' (1978-9). Acheampong revalued the Cedi and introduced price controls (which Nkrumah had tried previously). There was relative economic stability during Acheampong's first two years. Thereafter, his economic policies degenerated in practice into a virtually unbridled orgy of looting of the national treasury and the economy generally (Oquaye, 1980).

Concerned at the continuing balance of payments problem, Acheampong imposed import controls (Killick, 1983), but these provided another avenue for corruption and the 'parallel' market. In order to pay for the escalating price of oil after 1973 and to keep the trade unions as allies by providing jobs, Acheampong printed money and borrowed even more (Chazan, 1983, pp. 162-71). Government revenue from cocoa also decreased as cocoa farmers resorted to smuggling their cocoa out of the country in order to stabilize or increase their real income (Mufson, 1983).

While cocoa enjoyed a high price on the world market, the Ghanaian economy stagnated. Economic conditions were characterized by high inflation, increasing budget deficits, critical shortages of consumer goods and raw materials, corruption, price control evasion, tax evasion, participation in the world recession and deteriorating terms of trade (Novicki, 1984b, p. 43).

Following Acheampong's clumsy handling of the 'Unigov' attempt to hand over power to a mixed civilian/military/police regime, Akuffo took over in 1978. Akuffo's devaluation of the Cedi by 58 per cent won him labour unrest, the need to declare a state of emergency and $100 million in stand-by facilities from the IMF. This sum was inadequate to rehabilitate the economy. Further loans from the IMF, the World Bank and the EEC were to be conditional upon Akuffo further devaluing the Cedi (*AC*, **20**, No. 7, 28 March 1979, pp. 2–3). The official value of the Cedi was one-quarter of the black market rate. The budget deficit grew from $800 million to $900 million (*AC*, **19**, No. 25, 15 December 1978, p. 1). Akuffo was unable to control the corruption.

On 4 June 1979, the junior ranks of the armed forces freed Flight-Lieutenant J. J. Rawlings from prison, making him Chairman of the Armed Forces Revolutionary Council (AFRC, 4 June–24 September 1979). The AFRC executed a number of generals for corruption (these included former military junta heads, Afrifa, Acheampong and Akuffo). Numerous other officers, civil servants and business people were tried before the new Public Tribunals and given long prison sentences. In short, the main thrust of the first Rawlings government was to attempt a moral purge of the country's chief economic actors. The country's economic problems were seen to be mainly the result of the immoral actions of those in power: once morality, and the honour of the armed forces, were restored by the necessary moral purgatives, then the economy should recover. Rawlings at this point was something of a 'Robin Hood' nationalist.

Limann (1979–81) was unable to halt the economic rot. While gross domestic investment had decreased by an average of 3.2 per cent per year for the years 1960–70, from 1970 to 1980 the average decrease in gross domestic investment was nearly double (6.2 per cent). During the period 1970–80 the GDP fell by 0.1 per cent per year, the GNP fell by 1 per cent per year and industrial and agricultural production fell by 1.2 per cent per year. The wholesale price index climbed from 100 in 1975, to 555.9 in 1979, and to 796.4 in 1980. The consumer price index rocketed from 100 in 1975 to 903 at the end of 1979, to 1,335.4 in 1980, and more than doubled to 2,934.3 by Limann's overthrow on 31 December in the next year. Key consumer goods and medicines were usually only available on the black market at highly inflated prices. Ivory Coast's cocoa 'production' figures benefited from Ghanaian smuggling. The foreign exchange shortage became so critical that capital projects were stalled and the infrastructure suffered severe erosion (further details can be seen in the Basic Data section and in Chapter 1).

Limann's People's National Party was, like Nkrumah's CPP to which it claimed heritage, split between right and left wings. However, the dominant orientation was to the right, which was what the government's economic policies generally reflected. In as much as the Limann government was able to analyse these admittedly overwhelming problems, its solution was to try to attract foreign capital in two ways. Limann established a new foreign investment code as a mechanism for attracting foreign private capital capable of establishing new businesses, and producing jobs (see, for example, *AC*, **22**, No. 8, 8 April, 1981, p. 3). This new code opened up Ghana's economy to foreign profit-making. The government also entered into negotiations with the IMF in order to obtain the large amounts of foreign public capital necessary to rehabilitate the economic infrastructure. The IMF reputedly offered loans of US$130 million for the first year, together with US$900–950 million over the next three years. In return, the Limann government was expected to:

1. devalue the Cedi by 50 to 80 per cent.
2. increase the government's payments to farmers for cocoa by 300 per cent in order to stimulate the production of foreign-exchange generating cocoa;
3. increase interest rates;
4. remove controls on the importation and pricing of goods (apart from some fifteen 'essential' consumer goods;
5. reschedule and then repay foreign debts;
6. cut government expenditure (especially in services such as education) by various means, including firing 30,000 people from the civil service [*AC*, **22**, No. 8, 8 April, 1981, p. 3, and **23**, No. 1, 6 January 1982, pp. 4–6].

All these IMF conditions would have had political repercussions as well as the ostensible economic effect of making Ghana more productive. First, they would have turned Ghana's economy further away from a reliance on the public sector to provide certain social services and productive goods. Second, the IMF proposals would have aroused political opposition from many sectors of the population who saw their jobs or other interests threatened. The proposal to devalue the Cedi was especially explosive since the previous civilian government of Busia had been overthrown when it attempted to devalue. Certainly, Limann had reason to fear the fate of his government on this score.

The economic deterioration continued throughout Limann's final year in power. Food reserves were low: three months for rice and only ten days for corn. Most factories were operating at 20 per cent capacity because of the lack of foreign exchange to buy replacement parts and raw materials. According to one source, US$400 million in loans or investment would have been required to double this capacity, yet petroleum imports consumed US$100 million, which formed 80 per cent of total imports, or 40 per cent of foreign exchange earnings, which was four times the 1978 figure (Pagni, 1985, p. 30; see also Kraus, 1985, pp. 164–8; Kronholz, 1982). As Limann and other members of his government were rounded up in the early hours of the December 31st revolution, Rawlings and the other leaders faced a daunting task—economic recovery.

From the earliest days of the revolution there had been a division over political and economic strategies (see Chapter 4). The June Fourth Movement wanted a quick transition to a socialist society. Others on the left such as the New Democratic Movement also wanted this but doubted that the transition would be anything but a gradual move through the national democratic phase of the revolution. Others did not wish to proceed beyond that stage. At first, PNDC economic policy comprised general statements denouncing poverty, corruption and imperialism (Rawlings, 31 December 1981; PNDC, *Preamble*, May 1982; see also *Daily Graphic* and *Ghanaian Times*, January–February 1982), as well as a series of laws and initiatives designed to attack the wealthy (who were perceived to be corrupt) and defend the poor. The PNDC's May 1982 'Preamble to Policy Guidelines' reflected the early orientation, which in turn reflected dependency theory.

Ghana is not a poor country . . . The wealth of this country has been produced by the peasant farmers, fishermen and other working people, but the broad majority of the people have been denied the opportunity of using this wealth for the satisfaction of their requirements. . . . The [deposed] oligarchy lacked direction and the economy became uncontrollable under the weight of neo-colonialism which promotes local mismanagement, corruption and exploitation.

The question, however, was what was to be done about it? The revolution was 'to break the monotony of under-development', 'launch a fresh start in the task of national reconstruction', dismantle neo-colonial economic and political arrangements, etc. These statements were valid expressions of policy intent, but neither they nor the unpublished analysis and recommendations on the various sectors of economic and political life were linked to a detailed set of policy implementation steps. In short, there was an initial macro-policy orientation but not a coherent economic policy.

There was an early series of micro-level economic laws but these lacked coherence, integration and follow-up. Some black marketeers were attacked in the markets in a vain attempt to bring down the price of goods which were usually only available on the black market. Sometimes the houses and cars of those suspected of having obtained their wealth by corruption were seized, but sometimes, through bribery and other means, the wealthy managed to repossess them. The halls of free masonry and other wealthy elements were attacked, confiscated and handed over to political movements, defence committees and revolutionary youth groups on the grounds that these had been the gathering places of economic and political counter-revolutionaries, i.e. the rich.

In tandem with these actions, often lacking PNDC approval, a series of laws were passed to limit the power of the rich. The PNDC Establishment Proclamation (11 January 1982) removed the constitutional structures that had legitimized the wealthy's political control by suspending the old constitution. Another example was PNDC Law No. 1 (1 February 1982) which established the Citizens' Vetting Committee to investigate and punish private citizens found guilty of corruption, and tax evasion in particular. PNDC Law No. 2 (3 February 1982) was passed to deal with equivalent offenders in the public sector. PNDC Law No. 5 ('Rent Control', 12 March 1982) ordered landlords to stop exploiting their tenants. Landlords were to lower their rents by 50 per cent and not to charge more than twenty Cedis per month for a single room. PNDC Law No. 7 closed one loophole by which landlords tried to avoid rent control by not letting their premises: landlords were ordered to let all unoccupied houses or rooms. PNDC Law No. 6 tried to establish some degree of worker control over certain public boards and corporations by setting up Interim Management Committees which had four management representatives and three worker representatives (one from the trade union, two from the workers' defence committee).

All of this was designed to limit the economic power of one class alliance, enhance the power of the poor and the workers, and alleviate some of the suffering. However, in the form that they were formulated and implemented, they represented no more than pinpricks to the boils of the bourgeoisie—messy, some pain, but not a fundamental threat to their economic power. Economic problems continued to mount. The PNDC's first Secretary for Finance was not appointed until some months after the seizure of power, a sign of policy drift and disagreement within the PNDC. Rawlings became increasingly impatient with a situation that seemed to produce words but little economic improvement. The recovery programme had to lower inflation, unemployment and corruption.

The revolutionary government realized that if economic recovery was to take place, then production had to be increased. The key questions were: who was to produce it and how was increased production to be achieved. Whoever increased production needed foreign exchange to purchase from abroad a variety of equipment, spare parts and raw materials. Ghana's lack of an integrated economy had meant that its infrastructure and productive capacity depended for its maintenance on these foreign items. To undertake this rehabilitation, the PNDC needed massive amounts of capital.

PNDC member Chris Atim led a delegation to Eastern Europe in search of the necessary capital. While some economic assistance was forthcoming from the Soviet Union,[4] their limited foreign capital resources were already strained by prior commitments (Botchwey interview, Accra, 8 August 1984) to close allies such as Cuba, Afghanistan and Vietnam. The Ghanaian revolution was very much an unknown quantity to them: was Rawlings another initially uncommitted Castro or an ultimately hostile populist like Nasser? Besides the Eastern bloc countries, Libya was another non-Western source of aid for Ghana's revolution and she provided food and oil at the beginning of the revolution. According to one Western source, Rawlings' refusal to accept the stationing of Libyan troops in Ghana led to the Libyan refusal to provide more aid (Kraus, 1985, pp. 164–8), however, given the hysteria that usually surrounds even the mention of Libya in the Western press, this explanation is open to question. Given the decline in the global price of oil (Libya's main source of revenue) and Libya's involvement in the Chad civil war, Libya probably did not have the necessary huge quantities of capital.

Moreover, it was not just a question of access to capital but one of expertise and control which had to be considered. Libya did not have the technical expertise. The Soviet Union and its allies had the expertise but wanted guarantees that their projects would not be handed over to the Western powers, as had happened after Nkrumah's fall, for dismemberment and international ridicule. Large-scale economic aid from the Soviet Union would have signalled an adoption of the Soviet model of socialism that the PNDC could not have sustained. Since the PNDC did not fully control the civil service, the army, the peasantry or the trade unions, a contentious move of this kind would have been extremely difficult to implement.

Having gleaned what it could from the socialist and radical countries, the revolution had to turn elsewhere (Botchwey, interview, 8 August, 1984). Under the direction of Dr K. Botchwey, Secretary for Finance and Dr J. S. Abbey of the National Economic Recovery Commission (formerly Finance Adviser to Generals Acheampong and Akuffo), a four-year (1983–7) Economic Recovery Programme was planned in 1982. The programme was designed to lay the economic basis of the national democratic revolution. The PNDC's expectations were:

— to restore incentives for production of food, industrial raw materials and export commodities and thereby increase their output to modest but realistic levels;
— to increase the availability of essential consumer goods and improve the distribution system;
— to increase the overall availability of foreign exchange in the

country, improve its allocation mechanisms and channel it into selected high priority activities;
— to lower the rate of inflation by pursuing prudent fiscal, monetary and trade policies;
— to rehabilitate the physical infrastructure of the country in support of directly productive activities;
— to undertake systematic analyses and studies leading towards a major restructuring of the economic institutions in the country (PNDC, *Two Years*, 1984, pp. 24–5).

By mid-1982, the PNDC had started to approach the Western powers and the IMF for the capital needed to rehabilitate the export industries and their infrastructure that would eventually produce the capital needed for social services as well as consumer and production goods. On 20 October 1982 Dr Botchwey declared that Ghana was opening discussions with the IMF in order to secure credit to start implementing the economic recovery programme. The PNDC had been designing an economic package that would be realistic and so prevent the IMF from imposing 'unreasonable conditions' (Botchwey, interview, Accra, 8 August 1984 and PNDC, *Two Years*, 1984, p. 67). In response, some elements of the June Fourth Movement and the People's Revolutionary League of Ghana staged a peaceful attempted coup on 29 October (see Chapter 8). Its failure, together with that of 23 November 1982 resulted in the withdrawal of the most organized opposition within the PNDC to IMF loans.

After prolonged negotiations with the IMF and the World Bank, the PNDC was successful in negotiating a credit package of over $300 million. Having received the IMF's 'seal of approval', a number of bilateral and multilateral credit agreements with the West were concluded. The PNDC began to administer its part of the IMF agreement. In March 1983 the PNDC devalued the Cedi by over 1,000 per cent. The April 1983 budget sought to reduce the government's deficit by reducing government spending. In a country that had grown accustomed to imported goods and where the government was the largest employer, these measures were not well received. The trade union movement reacted sharply—a measure of the revolution's inability to control it.

The TUC contained pre-revolutionary as well as now-unsympathetic June Fourth Movement elements: indeed, the Workers' Defence Committees at Tema, to whom the abortive 29 October 1982 coup was announced, were among the most outspoken in their condemnation of the budget which reduced real wages and aggravated the food problems of the workers (see their statement in W.A., 5 May 1983, p. 1051). The student movement, NUGS, now under conservative control, also attacked the budget.

The price of cocoa was increased by 67 per cent in 1983, and again by 50 per cent in 1984 in order to encourage production and to earn foreign exchange. Price controls were gradually reduced—in fact they had never been successfully enforced—so that by the end of 1984 only twenty-three 'essential' goods were still covered by price controls. State subsidies were thus removed from many goods. Goods became more openly available but remained beyond the means of the average Ghanaian since the minimum salary, although raised from ¢12.50 per day in 1981 to ¢70 by December 1984, did not keep pace. Wage differentials shrunk as the higher-paid staff salaries in the public sector were not raised; this aided the government's plan to move workers from the civil service to the private and cooperative sectors. Interest rates were raised to promote a more efficient use of capital. Government spending was reduced in a further effort to fight inflation for the IMF: government deficits were nearly halved from 4.4 per cent of GDP in 1982 to 2.6 per cent in 1983 (Pagni, 1985, p. 37).

Despite numerous problems, the PNDC's economic strategy started to have some positive effect at the macro-level. Reversing the overall trend of the 1960s and 1970s, GNP actually rose by 0.7 per cent in 1983 and by 5.5 per cent in 1984. Had it not been for the intervention of nature, the GNP's increase might have been even higher. As it was, food scarcity was caused by drought, bushfires and the expulsion of a million Ghanaians from Nigeria (Ray, 1983). Bushfires destroyed many of the cocoa farms, leading to a sharp decrease in cocoa exports and therefore in foreign currency earnings. Foreign exchange earnings also dropped when the aluminium company VALCO was forced to reduce production because the drought had lowered the water level in the Akosombo dam and hence electricity output on which aluminium refining depends. These production problems were compounded by a transportation crisis induced by a lack of foreign exchange, as Ghana waited for IMF and World Bank disbursements, and by an accident at the single oil refinery: oil imports were reduced to 62 per cent (Kraus, 1985). Tractors, trucks and cars stood idle waiting for replacement parts, particularly tyres; queues for the weekly petrol ration lasted as long as three days and the illegal price of petrol was ten times the control price.

During 1983, over US$571 million was made available to the December 31st revolution for its recovery programme by a variety of Western-controlled foreign capital sources. Once the PNDC had received the stamp of legitimacy from the IMF and the World Bank, other donors made available a series of loans and grants. The IMF provided $255 million in standby credits and as much as $86 million in compensatory funds. The World Bank loaned to Ghana $90 million for the revival of the foreign-currency-generating exports of cocoa, gold and timber. The IMF's International Development Association provided a short-term bridging 'soft' loan of $40 million to be used to import materials and spare parts needed to rehabilitate the agricultural and transportation sectors of the economy. The Standard Chartered Bank made another short-term bridging loan for the imported needs of other economic sectors. In November 1983, at the World Bank donors' conference (Paris I), pledges amounting to $156 million for 1984 were received. However, the *de facto* premier, the PNDC Co-ordinating Secretary, stated that this was not enough. P. V. Obeng estimated that Paris I would result in a capital shortfall of $280 million for the years 1984 and 1985 (*West Africa*, 3 December 1984). Thus, by the end of 1984, Ghana's foreign capital requirements to rehabilitate its shattered economy were estimated by the PNDC, the IMF, etc. to comprise a minimum of US$1,007 million for the years 1983–5.

To what extent Ghana under the PNDC was forced or was not forced to accept IMF measures has been a matter of debate. Dr Botchwey has stated that Ghana decided on a type of financial pre-emptive strike by putting together a recovery package that did indeed contain elements of the standard IMF austerity packages, but which were designed and integrated into the Ghanaian reality by Ghanaians under the direction of the PNDC (Botchwey, interview, 8 August 1984). Consequently, state subsidies of consumer goods and parastatals as well as import and price controls were to be reduced, redesigned or eliminated, the Cedi was devalued by over 2,000 per cent of its 1981 value as of 1986, taxes were increased, public sector incomes were restrained and prices to agricultural producers were also increased.[5] In contrast to the early days of the revolution when the June Fourth Movement held power, foreign investment of certain types was encouraged if it was in the foreign-currency earning export sector.[6]

Criticism of the effects of the IMF programme mounted. Some argued that the benefit of increased credit mainly favoured the commercial sector. Multinational companies continued to avoid taxation. Unemployment was increased by redundancies in the public sector. This further reduced income and hence effective demand. The tax system was perceived as unjust, the poorest contributing the largest part of state revenues. Some 80 per cent of direct taxes were paid by the 12 per cent of the population who were wage- and salary-earners (*West Africa*, 26 March 1984, pp. 654–5; Abugri, 1983).

The PNDC recognized that it had been unable during 1983 to protect the average Ghanaian from the full impact of the IMF measures. Indeed, while the PNDC hoped that Ghanaians would begin to experience the benefits of the economy as it recovered, their expectation was that although the macro-performance had drastically improved by 1984, the ordinary Ghanaian would not feel the difference for several years. Consequently, the PNDC often found itself in conflict over wage demands with the labour movement, which was supposed to be part of the revolution's political base (Botchwey, interview, Accra, 8 August 1984; *West Africa*, 26 March, 1984, pp. 654–5). The question had become one of whether available capital resources should be directed towards production or consumption. This reflected the dilemma of the revolution: the necessity to revive capitalism because the political and economic structures of socialism were not there.

Throughout 1984, the PNDC continued to apply this economic strategy. They directed capital resources towards projects that generated foreign exchange, government revenue, or else increased the production of 'essential' consumer goods. The private sector's recovery was aided by the direction of 70 per cent of available new capital to it for the years 1984–6. The 1984 budget was orientated towards encouraging production and investment in Ghana. Government expenditure on development projects was to rise by 46 per cent. The duty on minerals was abolished. The export levy on gold was slashed to 6 per cent from 20 per cent. The tax rates on profits were increased. The PNDC was also able to take some measures to ease the burden on the poorer sections of the population; income tax for the lowest wage range was reduced, the minimum wage was increased by 60 per cent and the average civil service salary was raised by 40 per cent. These were significant increases in income given that inflation had slowed to 30 per cent in 1984, but of course the ravages of earlier inflation remained largely unaddressed (*Home Front*, **3**, No. 1, July 1984, p. 5).

Since most Ghanaian high-school students attended boarding schools they had been hard hit by the inflation in food prices of 1983. Indeed, many schools had been closed down early in the term because they lacked the food to feed their students. The 400 per cent increase in the feeding subsidy by the PNDC enabled the schools to overcome the problem.

The new foreign investment code was designed to attract new capital, expertise and jobs to the exhausted Ghanaian economy. Secretary of Finance Botchwey argued that the new code was designed to overcome earlier problems with foreign investors. Formerly, concessions and incentives had been given to foreign investment even when these projects contributed little innovation to Ghana's repertoire of technology and production. Previous codes did not encourage a renewal of foreign capital inflow but a recycling of the original profits so that increased foreign control of the Ghanaian economy was increasingly financed by Ghanaian economic opportunities. Furthermore, foreign investors then demanded the right not only to repatriate their own capital but also to take with them the capital that had accrued to them from their Ghanaian business. Thus, foreign investment had previously often resulted in a net capital drain on the economy rather than an addition to the country's capital stock.

Accordingly, more foreign capital was to be attracted into Ghana by allowing companies that were net foreign-exchange earners to freely export foreign exchange out of Ghana in order to remit dividends and debt service payments. These foreign investors were further required to invest a minimum of $100,000 in the new Ghanaian company as well as employing at least twenty-five Ghanaians. Joint foreign–Ghanaian ventures were to be initially 40 per cent foreign-financed. Such measures, Botchwey argued, would ensure that foreign investment would increase the export sector by introducing new capital, new technology, new jobs and new production, while at the same time allowing foreign investors to make profits, though not at the expense of Ghana's sovereignty (*Home Front*, 3, No. 1, July 1984, p. 20).

Having initially been 'blessed' by the IMF in 1983, the bilateral and multilateral benefits continued to flow into Ghana during 1984. Grants amounted to US$148 million and loans to US$172 million for a total of a 1984 foreign capital institutional inflow of US$320 million (*People's Daily Graphic*, 24 December 1984). Thus, in the first two years of the IMF's approval, the PNDC gained access to US$891 million for its economic recovery programme. In 1984, multilateral funds were directed into agricultural exports and the transportation infrastructure. Mining, timber, industrial rehabilitation, water and transport all benefited from western bilateral agreements. Bilateral and multilateral sources also gave $70 million in food aid. The Eastern bloc provided technical and financial assistance to industry as well as bridging loans for the balance of payments (*People's Daily Graphic*, 24 December 1984).

Agriculture continued during 1984 to pose a problem for the PNDC. The replanting of cocoa trees continued in an effort to reverse the decline in production as the older trees stopped producing. Food crops benefited from better rainfall in 1984 but it was still necessary to import cereals, fish and vegetables worth ¢240 million (*West Africa*, 3 September 1984, 1972). The price of maize fell from a range of ¢14,000 to ¢3,000 per bag in 1983 to as low as ¢800 in 1984. This drop in the price of food greatly benefited the urban consumer, but, conversely, put pressure on the farmers.

Overall, agricultural policy, apart from a desire to boost foreign-exchange earning cocoa, continued to drift in both economic and political terms. The agricultural service remained out of the PNDC's control but wedded to large-scale farmers who had mechanized. The vast majority of farmers who operated small farms but produced most of the food were effectively ignored by the service. The PNDC did not develop a political strategy for mobilizing its natural constituency among the farmers, i.e. agricultural workers as well as poor and middle-income farmers. There was some discussion of cooperatives and communal self-help projects, but little was done. The major reason for this was that there was little available in the way of political resources, most of these being devoted to maintaining control of the centre and achieving the macro-levels of the economic recovery programme. Consequently, there was little revolutionary organization carried out in the countryside aside from salvage operations with some defence committees.

Economically, the PNDC were able to squeeze some initiatives from this dry political situation. The EEC agreed to supply over US$200 million in agricultural inputs to be distributed through a new system of local rural banks in an effort by the PNDC to get credit and inputs to those who actually produced. Realizing that the agricultural service's estimates of producers and production were to a large extent fictional, the PNDC directed that a national agricultural sample census be conducted in 1985. In fairness to the agricultural service, it must be noted that their guesstimates were a result of Acheampong's looting of the national treasury which destroyed the civil service's ability to gather information, and also that the last such census had been conducted in 1970. The PNDC urged that small-scale irrigation projects be built across the country in order to combat future droughts. Like the idea of establishing a series of food silos to create food reserves, this remained a concept of great merit, though with little likelihood of being implemented quickly owing to a lack of capital, expertise and political will in senior political and administrative circles (Pagni, 1985, pp. 29–34; *West Africa*, 3 September 1984, pp. 1,772–73).

More goods became available as 1984 progressed, but there were still consumer goods shortages of soap, paraffin, and cloth in rural areas (women were frequently seen wearing army fatigue trousers). In the urban areas, a wide range of goods suddenly appeared after the price controls were no longer enforced in places. These goods were very expensive. Despite their inability mostly to purchase them, however, many Ghanaians seemed to gather encouragement from their mere appearance.

Significantly, the PNDC's economic recovery programme succeeded at the macro-level. After the downhill slide of the 1960s and 1970s, the GDP rallied in 1983 by actually increasing by 0.07 per cent

In 1984 the GDP increased by an amazing 5.5 per cent (*People's Daily Graphic*, 12 January 1985). This estimate was consistent with the World Bank's earlier estimates (interview, Accra, July 1984).

During 1985 and 1986, the PNDC's economic policies continued much as they had since 1983, the main focus being the attraction of foreign capital. In a further effort to attract foreign capital into timber and mining, the government announced that its approval would not be required for non-sterling zone currencies (*West Africa*, 8 April 1985, p. 687).

Finance Secretary Botchwey announced in the 1985 budget that US$950 million would be used to import much-needed materials to activate such key economic sectors as transport, communications, fuel, industry, construction, cocoa and other agricultural as well as food imports. Expenditure and revenue were increased by 76 per cent, with expenditure on development being sharply increased to one-quarter from one-sixth of the total. The budget had been influenced by the newly-established National Economic Commission. This was chaired by PNDC member, Justice Annan. The Vice-Chairman was P. V. Obeng, PNDC Co-ordinating Secretary. Other members included Finance Secretary Botchwey, Dr J. S. Abbey (together with Botchwey, one of the founders of Ghana's IMF strategy), as well as Frank Annor, Anthony Kobina Wood and a number of business leaders (*People's Daily Graphic*, 19 April 1985; *Ghana News*, **13**, No. 12, December 1984, p. 8).

The second donor's conference resulted in pledges of $58 million for 1985 as well as an estimated US$750 from the IMF and the World Bank for the years 1985–7. The provision of this capital was reputedly dependent on Ghana devaluing the Cedi by another 30 per cent to $1 = ¢53 and on the abandonment of the interim management committees. The PNDC conducted the necessary devaluation. It tried to soften the blow to workers by doubling the minimum wage. However, this was partially undercut by the 50 per cent rise in the price of kerosene, which hit the rural population very hard, and by the 25 per cent rise in the price of gasoline, which caused hardship to low-paid urban workers (*AC*, **25**, No. 20, 30 October 1984, No. 25, 12 December 1984, p. 3).

The PNDC also dismantled the Interim Management Committees,

which had been a revolutionary vehicle for giving workers a say in the running of various companies and units.[6] These operational committees were replaced by Joint Consultative Committees which were downgraded to an advisory role to management. Managers were not obliged to follow this advice, but assumed complete responsibility for the firm or unit's progress (*AC*, **25**, No. 24, 12 December 1984, p. 3).

At first glance this might seem to mark the final surrender of the revolution on the labour front and a return to pre-revolutionary days.[7] However, a number of factors have to be taken into consideration here. It did mark a retreat, but a retreat forced on the PNDC by the lack of organized workers under the direction of the PNDC and by the economic strategy itself. The recovery programme depended on access to large pools of capital, which only the IMF and the World Bank controlled (Botchwey, interview, Accra, 8 August 1984). These sources demanded that their funds be used by managers for 'technical' purposes and that there should not be 'political' interference from the workers. For the moment, the PNDC was too weak economically and politically to argue with the IMF's reasoning which 'just' happened to favour the managers and business owners. Moreover, given that the revolution was perceived by its leaders to be in the national democratic phase, such a move was seen as not only one that had been forced on Ghana, but also one necessary for internal political and economic reasons. Managers needed to be reassured that they were still needed and welcome in Ghana during the revolution if they were to boost production and if some of them were to be won over to socialism in the long run. In the short run, these measures, together with the transformation of people's and worker's defence committees into Committees for the Defence of the Revolution were designed to put some reality into the phrase 'national democratic phase of the revolution' by removing obstacles to the involvement of the nationalist elements of the business and professional classes.

These changes reflected the dissatisfaction that Rawlings and other elements of the revolutionary leadership had felt with the weak revolutionary structures for the workers that had mainly been the inspiration of those elements of the June Fourth Movement involved in the attempted coup against Rawlings. By the end of 1982, this attempted coup had highlighted the other problems experienced by the workers' and people's defence committees. The leadership was often enthusiastic, sometimes corrupt, but usually inexperienced and with little access to the resources that would develop their growing experience into an ability to create a revolutionary movement. The revolution had nearly foundered as Rawlings and the NDM discovered that the defence committees were not as reliable as they would have liked. New structures were needed, but economic problems seemed ready to overwhelm the revolution during 1983. When workers, led by their defence committees, disrupted production, as in the Pioneer Canning Company 1984 strike and lock-out in Tema, the political unreliability of the structures themselves was increased.

The workers' defence committees had been established because the June Fourth Movement and others had become suspicious of the existing trade union movement, the Trades Union Congress, but had lacked the strength to set up their own union movement. The workers' defence committees were thus to act as watchdogs over the TUC and the nuclei of the working class cells of a new revolutionary party. When the workers' defence committees proved in certain key areas to be politically unreliable and disruptive of production, thus creating problems in the IMF's eyes, their days were numbered. So the PNDC retreated. The workers' defence committees were reined in and transformed. Worker participation in managing their units was reduced to an advisory role. As in the Soviet Union after the revolutionary seizure of power, workers' organizations were ordered to increase production in order to provide the economic base for the revolution. Having re-organized their labour policy, the PNDC hoped to clean up the mess and move afresh to create new revolutionary vehicles, including the retraining of defence committee cadres at a new revolutionary school. From this, a new political base could be established. While waiting for that to happen, the PNDC continued to view economic recovery as the top priority, and rearranged other policies in that light.

The PNDC has been criticized for this strategy. It has been argued that, under IMF tutelage, Ghana's export sector will be restored, but not coordinated with Ghana's other sectors such as other raw materials, energy, industries and human resources, in order to produce an integrated economy (*West Africa*, 2 March 1984; Abugri, 1983). The PNDC has become to some extent dependent for its stability on the continuing inflow of capital. In the short term, some of the conditions imposed by foreign agencies and governments did bring hardship for many Ghanaians, but a serious threat to stability did not emerge because of it. Moreover, the IMF's programme has not had a record of consistent successes. The IMF's successes have been mainly with the more economically developed Asian countries with a different resource mix than in Africa. Of the IMF patients, only 20 per cent have achieved their growth-rate goals, and less than one half have met their inflation and balance of payments goals (*West Africa*, 11 March 1985, p. 456). Moreover, the question has been raised by a variety of sources, but especially the June Fourth Movement, as to whether the IMF has been used by the United States to undermine socialism around the world. Indeed, the United States would like to do so: the US Treasury has stated that:

The multilateral development banks by and large have been the most effective in furthering our global economic and financial objectives and thereby also serve our long-term political/strategic objectives. . . . Neither bilateral assistance nor private sector flows if available are as effective in influencing less developed countries' economic performance as the multilateral development banks [*West Africa*, 2 April 1984, p. 709.]

By contrast, by adopting an economic recovery programme that contains, among other trends, elements of Lenin's NEP and Mao's national democratic phase of the revolution, the PNDC has been able to mobilize the enormous sums of foreign capital needed to get the economy going again. By the beginning of 1985, the GDP growth was being projected at over 5 per cent—in sharp contrast to the decline of the 1960s and 1970s. The issue of the IMF loans is not whether they are acceptable to socialist governments—Chile under Allende, Grenada, Jamaica under Manley, Tanzania and Nicaragua have all wanted loans from the IMF and the World Bank—but rather at what cost. That cost will not emerge for some time. In the meantime, Ghana under the PNDC became a modest but real economic macro-level success story

Foreign Policy

As a British colony, Ghana automatically followed British policy, finding itself at war when Britain declared it. Throughout the two world wars (1914–18 and 1939–45), Ghanaians fought bravely. After the Second World War, Ghanaians found that their country, as part of the British Empire, was automatically embroiled in the cold war of the capitalist powers against communism—notably against that variety of communism espoused by the Soviet Union and its emerging allies. During the period of the dyarchy (1951–7), Nkrumah began to loosen British control over foreign policy and to prepare the way for an independent foreign policy.

After independence in 1957, Nkrumah developed a foreign policy that emphasized African freedom and unity, non-alignment, and membership of the Commonwealth and the United Nations. While he sought to establish socialism in Ghana, he actively courted the Western and Eastern powers for financial resources and assistance. He established relations with the Eastern bloc countries and their allies, thus breaking the 'cordon sanitaire' which the British had imposed around Ghana. He helped create the Organization of African Unity in 1963. Besides sowing the seeds of continental unity, Nkrumah attempted to establish a federation with Mali and Guinea as well as giving political and material support to the freedom movements in various European-colonized countries in Africa (Thompson, 1969; Addo, 1978; Price, 1967). Like his successors in the PNDC, his foreign policy emphasized nationalism and a search for resources with which to build a progressive future.

The NLC (1966–9), which was the military junta that overthrew Nkrumah, moved quickly to break relations with the Soviet Union and its allies. Eastern-funded projects came to a halt. The NLC abandoned the policy of non-alignment and moved firmly into the camp of the United States and Britain (Bluwey, 1976; Addo, 1978). The elected civilian government of Prime Minister Busia (1969–72) continued with these policies (Bluwey, 1967; Addo 1978; Chazan, 1983). The military governments of General Acheampong (1972–8) opened diplomatic and trade relations with the Soviet Union, re-emphasised African unity (marked by Ghana being one of the founders of

ECOWAS—the Economic Community of West African States), and efforts to renegotiate and increase its debt burden with the World Bank, the United States, Canada and Western Europe, in order to fund the government's economic programme. Chazan notes that in this respect the Acheampong governments were like all their predecessors (Chazan, 1983, p. 167; see also Bluwey, 1976). Indeed, its successors (Akuffo, 1978–79; Limann, 1979–81 and the PNDC) have also followed this practice.

The first Rawlings government (the AFRC, 4 June–24 September 1979) moved further into non-alignment. Rawlings attended the Non-Aligned Movement's conference in Cuba where he met Castro. The AFRC opened up relations with Libya (Rawlings, interview, Accra, 7 August 1984; Okeke, 1982). President Limann's government changed its foreign policy orientation (Chazan, 1983) more towards the right of centre, though not to the same extent as Busia had done. Limann broke relations with Libya but maintained them with the Soviet Union and its allies. This reflected the dominance of the right in Limann's party, the PNP, but also the sizeable minority assortment of 'progressives' in the party.

The PNDC also contained widely divergent political trends. Unlike Limann, Rawlings moved Ghana more firmly into a policy of non-alignment. The PNDC's foreign policy[8] reflected this, and it can be divided into two phases. The first phase only lasted from the seizure of power on 31 December 1981 to the late middle of 1982. This coincided with the participation of all elements of the June Fourth Movement in the revolution. Reflecting their desire to move immediately on to socialism and communism, and their expectation that significant aid would be immediately forthcoming, these PNDC leaders regularly denounced imperialism, capitalism, the IMF, the World Bank, the Unitd States and Western Europe as seeking to entrap Ghana and as being the root cause of poverty in Ghana. By contrast, favourable evaluations were made of the Soviet Union and its allies, especially Cuba. However, the inability and/or reluctance of these socialist states to provide much aid following the visit of Chris Atim (then PNDC member) to Eastern Europe undermined the economic base of their revolutionary strategy that expected a quick move to socialism.

As the economy continued to collapse around the feet of the PNDC, and given the inability of the June Fourth Movement to get the necessary capital from the Eastern bloc countries and Libya, other forces came to dominate the PNDC's foreign policy. These included both Marxists, such as the New Democratic Movement, and liberals such as Dr J. S. Abbey. They both concluded that no form of revolution was likely to occur until the economic deterioration had halted and regeneration had begun. They both concluded that large elements of the state sector were uncontrollable in the short term and had performed poorly in recent times. Nevertheless, a programme of throwing out the dead wood and revitalizing the state sector was possible, but only if it went hand-in-hand with diverting much of the private sector out of illegality and into legality, the inducements involving both rewards (e.g. access to foreign currency) and punitive action (tax investigations). This mixed-economy strategy with a strong private sector component was necessary if the PNDC hoped to win the approval of the capitalist West which controlled the vast bulk of available multilateral and bilateral capital aid. Thus, for internal and external political and economic reasons, the PNDC reshaped its foreign policy to establish good relations with all states, especially those that were or could be important donors or lenders of the capital necessary to regenerate the economy. Accordingly, the PNDC publicly turned a blind eye to the links between the United States and West Germany and to several attempted coups. The PNDC only raised the issue publicly in the United States when, in 1985, Rawlings' cousin was arrested and accused of 'turning' an acknowledged CIA agent in the US Embassy.

Overall, the PNDC has sought to maintain a balance between the various countries in the major power blocs. In contrast to the earlier phase of the revolution, all public statements by PNDC members and Secretaries have, with few exceptions, refrained from taking an invective tone. Assistance, from whatever source, has been publicly and gratefully acknowledged.

Latin America has become a new focus of foreign policy activity. This new engagement has resulted in a breaking out from the old Commonwealth/European/United States primary mould. Although of secondary importance, Ghana's increasing involvement in Latin

America has reflected several factors. As a debtor nation and as a member of the African, Caribbean and Pacific country associates of the EEC, Ghana shared a certain number of common economic problems with them. Cuba, Nicaragua and (until 1983) Grenada were a series of friendly revolutionary states that provided examples of how-to and how-not-to proceed. Cuba also provided economic assistance to Ghana—especially expertise in the area of sugar production. Rawlings was impressed by what the Cubans had achieved in material terms, though his determined nationalism has led him to declare that he will follow no foreign model: Ghanaians must determine their own way forward in response to their own situation. These Ghanaian–Latin American relationships have been expanded by the 1979 and 1984 visits by Rawlings and other senior leaders to Cuba, Nicaragua (1984), Guyana (1984) and Surinam (1984).

A consistent theme of revolutionary foreign policy has been strong condemnation of racist apartheid in South Africa and Namibia. Unlike Busia's short-lived initiative to the South African government, the PNDC has provided political support for the liberation movements. Interestingly, one stamp issued under PNDC direction portrays soldiers of SWAPO (the South West African People's Organization of Namibia) on patrol against racism. Ghana has played a leading role in the Organization of African Unity's Liberation Committee which directs support to the liberation movements. In part this reflects the personal commitment of PNDC Chairman Rawlings and PNDC member Tsikata, but also the outlook of the left and liberal nationalists in Ghana which in turn has been part of Nkrumah's heritage. For example, in 1963, Captain Kojo Tsikata was sent to Congo-Brazzaville by Nkrumah to provide military training for the then fledgeling MPLA. This nationalist movement sought the freedom of Angola from Portuguese imperialism.

Closer to home, Ghana under the PNDC has often seen its relations with neighbouring states bedevilled by tension, if not outright hostility. The Nigerian Generals have had reservations about Rawlings since his first regime shot eight Ghanaian generals for severe corruption—a bad example for Nigerian junior ranks. The corrupt civilian regime of President Shagari suddenly expelled from Nigeria one million Ghanaians in an effort to find scapegoats for Nigeria's economic problems. This created major economic disruption in Ghana and considerably strained Ghana's relations with Nigeria. Ghana's response was remarkably guarded, perhaps a function of the fact that Ghana depended on Nigerian oil. Relations with Ivory Coast have been cordial but un-enthusiastic, a reflection of the difference in political outlook of the two countries and Ivory Coast's inability to control its border with Ghana. Relations with Togo have been greatly strained by Togo's habit of apparently harbouring Ghanaians planning and carrying out attempted coups against the PNDC. Since the seizure of power by Captain T. Sankura in Burkina Faso (formerly Upper Volta) on 4 August 1983, the personal friendship of Rawlings, the similarity of revolutionary circumstances and the desire for allies and friendly borders has led to increasing cooperation between the two countries. Joint military and political exercises have been held in what may emerge as some kind of federal system. Again, this has echoed Nkrumah's vision.

Other Domestic Policies: Education, Culture, Religion, Military Affairs and Women's Rights

An examination of other domestic policies such as those dealing with education, culture, religion, military affairs and women's rights illus-trates the obstacles that confronted the December 31st revolution.

The revolutionary leadership criticized pre-revolutionary educa-tion:[9]

The historical background to the present system shows that no comprehen-sive public educational policy has ever been fully pursued in this country. The aim of the colonial educational policy was to satisfy colonial interests, to disparage the African character and to service the colonial heritage. The late Dr. Kwame Nkrumah deserves credit for his great vision for democratic and nationalistic education, but this could not be realised. The result is that the present system, from the first cycle through University, is totally inadequate, expensive and useless. It has also favoured mostly the rich and the well-placed [PNDC, 1982, 83].

The revolutionary leadership thus used a framework of neo-Marixst dependency as a critique of the educational system under British occupation and under the post-Nkrumah but pre-revolutionary governments (1966–81). The variety of public, private and religious schools had mainly been modelled on the British system of producing an elite in the British image to the relative neglect of the majority. The PNDC made the accusation—to some considerable extent justified—that a large portion of public money had gone to increase the class divide and cultural alienation, as Fanon had predicted would happen in colonial and neo-colonial situations. Indeed, a well-trained intellectual and professional class that was the pride of much of Africa had been produced, but their contribution to national life had been somewhat lessened by their elitism.

Beyond this, there was the question of how educational resources were distributed. The concept of urban bias (Elliot, 1975) also applied to the case of Ghanaian education. Those from the urban areas in the south had the best access to a good education. The rural areas, and especially the north, were neglected. Indeed, Nkrumah even abolished fee-paying state schools in the north in order to overcome this earlier bias. Given that the PNDC felt the educational system did not serve the needs of the majority of the people—i.e. workers and peasants—and that it created and/or reinforced a process that divorced Africans from their continental heritage and tried to make them into black-skinned British, what was the PNDC to do?

In the immediate aftermath of the revolutionary seizure of power, the PNDC responded by developing a certain 'basic policy orientation'. Since they believed that education was a social responsibility that could only be carried out if it was free of elitism, the profit motive and religious conversion, state control was necessary. Students were no longer to be taught values that alienated them from their African and specifically Ghanaian heritage. Revolutionary education was to be orientated towards solving problems creatively and scientifically rather than the mere acquisition of a ticket that was of little use except to admit the bearer into the élite (PNDC, 1982, p. 24).

These prescriptions necessitated changes in the curriculum, teacher training, educational administration, the distribution pattern of educational resources as well as the general outlook of the educational system. However, the human, financial and political resources necessary to implement such policy goals were not present. The resource base of all levels of education had been seriously eroded by the economic crisis of the 1960s, 1970s, and early 1980s. Once the 'Oxford' of Africa, the University of Ghana was unable to buy foreign books or spare parts for its micro-film machines because of the lack of foreign currency. By 1983, professors' salaries were insufficient to feed their families. The primary and secondary schools lacked most of the materials needed to conduct their programmes. Many rural primary schools lacked desks, chairs, books and writing materials, except for a small amount of chalk for the teachers. Over 10,000 teachers and professors left the country, many going to Nigeria. The teaching profession and the professoriat were more than decimated by the economic crisis. Novice teachers with inferior qualifications partially filled the gaps (in one admittedly extreme case, the novice teacher did not know that London was the capital of Britain). Moreover, a good number of teachers left their jobs to work full-time in political and administrative positions in the revolution. For example, a number of teachers were seconded to the full-time executives of the regional, district and zonal defence committees. Other teachers and professors became PNDC Secretaries, etc.

The PNDC has therefore been unable to effect a major transformation of education for three main reasons: funds were not available; many teachers had left; and most importantly, many of the teachers with a revolutionary outlook had either been overburdened by the lack of resources and the depletion in the number of teachers or else had been siphoned off to work elsewhere in the revolution. The lack of politically-developed cadres has once more nearly hamstrung the implementation of the revolution's policies.

As with the economy, the first talk of 'revolution for education' did not turn out as expected, and was more a question of stabilizing the health of the educational system. A number of minor innovations were possible. The most notable of these were programmes to send Ghanaian students to study in the universities and technical colleges of Eastern Europe as well as to a high school in Cuba. Beginning in 1983, Cuba agreed to pay for the cost of educating over six hundred Ghanaian high-school students and their teachers at a school in Cuba.

Although this was initially opposed in some circles, many Ghanaian students eagerly grasped this opportunity to at least receive a secondary-school education. The creation of the Tamale Youth Home was another corrective measure.

Cultural policy has been based on a similar theoretical construct. Culture was seen by the December 31st revolution in the same light as the revolutionaries in Guinea-Bissau (Cabral 1977/8) had seen it: culture was a weapon against imperialism. The PNDC had two main areas of concern. First, the negative aspects of foreign culture had been undermining indigenous culture. Second, the Ministry of Culture and Tourism lacked the initiative to develop Ghanaian culture. Too often the Ministry had regarded its task as that of 'just signing cultural agreements'.

While the PNDC appreciated the need to critically evaluate Ghanaian culture, it argued that, too often, negative foreign cultural influences had been grafted into Ghanaian life by their financial backing, at the expense of local art forms. For example, indigenous music consisted of traditional and hi-life forms, but these were disappearing in the face of American music with its access to money, its endless advertising and attendant sense of prestige which changed consumer tastes. Ghanaians were becoming consumers of capitalist culture. Increasingly, in cultural circles, 'the echoing of foreign ideas' had been leading to a 'state of barrenness and apemanship' in what was left of Ghanaian culture. Ghanaians were being alienated from their culture by the uncontrolled invasion of capitalist culture. This was seen as part of the neo-colonial dependency relationship into which previous governments—that of Nkrumah being excepted—had helped to lead Ghana.

The second problem was more amenable to solution. The Minister was to cooperate with other ministries such as Education and Trade in order to integrate Ghanaian culture into education and job creation. This would be possible if the PNDC had 'the support of the masses of our people', but it recognized that a lack of the necessary financial and politicized human resources would hamper the mobilization of that support (PNDC 1982, pp. 39–42).

Despite the PNDC taking a 'cautious' approach to the question of religion (PNDC 1982, p. 42), much of the wealthier hierarchy of the major Christian Churches initially displayed its dislike of a revolutionary government to such an extent that the Church hierarchies' commitment to social justice was called into question. The Roman Catholic Church conducted a mini-purge of pro-revolutionary elements. Of course there was a certain sectarian attitude among some revolutionary elements, a number of whom left the regime after the attempted coups of October and November 1982. The fact that liberation theology is little-known or practised in Ghana has meant that, unlike the Nicaraguan revolution, few organic links developed between the Churches' members and the revolution to help counterbalance hostility to the hierarchy.

The PNDC did remove commercial religion from the airwaves, but continued to allow the broadcasting of religious programmes and music (*Legon Observer*, March 1982, p. 63). These programmes include a balance between Christianity and Islam. Religious affiliation and its public manifestation permeates Ghanaian society to such an extent that any national democratic and indeed socialist phases of the revolution must of necessity acknowlege local beliefs. The PNDC has done this. It has reflected not only the local balance of power, but genuine conviction on the part of senior members of the revolution such as Rawlings. As a young man, he had wanted to become a priest in order to be able to create social justice. There is a perception that Christianity and Islam contain revolutionary principles of social justice. Liberation theology had therefore perhaps had a more significant impact on the senior levels of the revolution than on their equivalent in the Churches. Revolutionary Islam has been percolating through Ghana, and has had its impact on the revolution.

With regard to military affairs, the December 31st revolution benefited from the 4 June 1979 uprising. The officer corps as a coherent group or class had been broken up by this uprising. Their collective power had been their ability to order their troops into action. For this, the officer corps had received considerable financial and promotional rewards from the Ghanaian state. They formed the military counterpart of the old ruling élite, but the corruption of the officers who had gathered around General Acheampong eroded this political standing. The 4 June uprising ended most of what remained (Annan, Accra, 4 August 1984). Thereafter, an officer's control of his unit depended in large measure on his own personal qualities. After 31 December 1981 the officers faced many of the same problems experienced by tsarist officers in the Russian army after the Bolsheviks seized power in October 1917. The key issue was: should the officers try to overthrow, to join the revolution, or just stay neutral?

In Ghana most officers had been neutralized by their loss of authority during the 4 June uprising. A few tried to overthrow the PNDC, but were never able to break out of their political, military and class isolation. The defence committees for the other ranks in the armed forces and police ensured this relative isolation of officers by acting as an alternative source of authority to the officers, as agents of revolutionary education, mobilization and action, and by acting as an intelligence network that reported coup plots to PNDC security for appropriate action (see, for example, *Legon Observer*, 12 February 1982, pp. 46–7). Thus, the PNDC's first concerns for military policy were to consolidate political support through the defence committees, to prevent coherent opposition from emerging within the military and to retain control of key units willing to defend the revolution.

Attempts were also made to involve the military in development projects. These varied from helping to repair sanitation systems, to repairing roads, to growing their own food (*Ghanaian Times*, 15 January 1985; *People's Daily Graphic*, 17 January 1984). An Army Borehole Drilling Unit was formed in the Field Engineer battalion to provide water for the rural population, thus supplementing the drilling units of the Ghana Water and Sewerage Corporation as well as those of the Canadian International Development Agency and West Germany (*Ghana News*, **14**, No. 1, January 1985, p. 12).

The PNDC also addressed the question of democratizing the military. Efforts were made to improve the conditions of the police and Army ranks (e.g., *People's Daily Graphic*, 2 November 1984), whose neglect had made a number of officers notorious. Soldiers who captured financial criminals such as smugglers were given promotion (*People's Daily Graphic*, 15 December 1984). Rawlings proposed that 40 per cent of the intake into the officer corps should consist of men and women from the ranks (WA, 29 November 1982, p. 3111). Units of a 'People's Militia', under Army command, were established.

The civil service was demoralized, lacked internal direction, and it was in some part unsympathetic to the PNDC. Lacking a revolutionary party, the PNDC resorted to the use of politically reliable members of the military to gain more control of the civil service. A Military Task Force was established to this end. In addition, the Committee of Secretaries (cabinet) ordered Armed Forces personnel to be seconded to ministerial advisory committees (*Ghana News*, **14**, No. 3, March 1985, p. 10).

The PNDC noted that, despite some aspects of the history of the Armed Forces and the Police, they still had key roles to fulfil in the revolution. PNDC Chairman Rawlings stated:

The Armed Forces and the Police came to us as a colonial legacy. They were instruments of oppression, and even now we have not entirely eradicated the attitudes of antagonism between the public and the men in uniform.

It has been one of the tasks of the revolution to break through these barriers of these attitudes, so that the forces see themselves as defenders of the people, and the people see them as colleagues and helpers. [Interview, Accra, 7 August, 1984.]

Ghana has larger armed forces than its neighbours. Joint exercises have been held by the forces of anglophone Ghana and francophone Burkina Faso as friendly ties have grown between the two revolutions.

While the revolution has tried to create women's organizations that will liberate women, the lack of resources and the youth of the revolutionary organizations have greatly hindered these efforts at change.[10] Nevertheless, Rawlings stated that the revolution has affirmed that social justice necessarily includes an end to the exploitation and oppression of all women. Women in Ghana, as in the rest of the world, are expected to live split lives: 'They may be educated and hold responsible jobs, and yet still be expected to conform to outmoded conceptions of a woman's place in society.' While some legal advances had been made, for example equal pay for work of equal value, there was much room for improvement. Hence, the PNDC has enacted laws to deal with problems such as inheritance for women and 'outmoded customs relating to widowhood'. However, the root of their problem is the attitude of men. Women's confidence in their leadership qualities has often been undermined by men because of their conservative attitudes. As mentioned earlier, even revolutionary men have been guilty of leaving their principles at their own front door:

Young men who declare themselves to be committed revolutionaries and who talk at length about liberation of the oppressed are often shocked if they are asked to think of their wives in these terms. Women wishing to take part in PDC [People's Defence Committees], cadre training courses, etc. are often made to feel guilty for not being at home cooking and looking after children. Few husbands would take time from educating factory workers or illiterate farmers to educate their own womenfolk! [Interview, Accra, 7 August, 1984.]

Thus, the changing of men's attitudes is most important, but once more the lack of resources with which to carry out the necessary education has greatly limited the implementation of the PNDC's policies. This limitation will most likely remain until the economic crisis has been significantly reduced and more revolutionary cadres have been trained.

In the interim, the emergence of a number of powerful women in the revolution as PNDC Members, Secretaries and top advisers to Rawlings, as well as Rawlings' positive attitude to women as full participants in society, the attempts to reform the law and to involve women in new opportunities for public decision-making, all are evidence of the PNDC's intentions for the future of women in Ghana.

9 Conclusions: Ghana in the Typology of Social Transformation

The Ghanaian revolution is part of what can now be identified as a new pattern of revolution. As Szajkowski (1985) has pointed out, there has been a tendency for scholars to be mesmerized by the admittedly awesome presence of the Soviet Union and, consequently, to try to jam every regime and movement into that mould. As he has noted, there are different forms of socialist revolution. Moreover, they have continued to evolve in response to changing global and local situations.

Szajkowski (1982, p. 155) argues that there have been three main periods in the establishment of Marxist regimes. The first period (1917–38) was centred around the 1917 Bolshevik Revolution in Russia and its aftermath. Efforts were made to emulate this first Soviet model in a number of Eastern European, Asian and Latin American countries, all of which failed or were incorporated into the Soviet Union. The second major period (1939–58) contained the events of the Second World War (1939–45) and its aftermath. Attempts were made to establish sister regimes in China, Yugoslavia, Vietnam, Albania, Bulgaria, Romania, Czechoslovakia, Korea, Poland, Hungary, Germany, Finland and Iran. All of these succeeded to some extent except Finland and Iran. Vietnam was divided for some time; Germany and Korea remain so. The Chinese and Vietnamese revolutions can be seen as being part of the transition to the third period—national liberation. They occurred in the context of growing Soviet power and assistance to other revolutions but they were also based on the concept of national democratic struggles that were prolonged, and that utilized the mobilization of a large proportion of the population for political and military activity.

Revolutions in the third period (1959–79) usually mixed nationalism, anti-imperialism and Marxism in an equation that varied from country to country, and within each country, on the basis of historical progression. All were organized on the model of 'a broad national democratic front in which [the Marxist–Leninist party] and other left-wing and liberal groups could participate' (Szajkowski, 1982, p. 124

passim). The actual revolutionary impetus had been transferred from Europe to the Third World as anti-colonial, anti-imperialist and nationalist movements grew in response to global changes in power such as the decay of the old empires and their eclipse by the United States and the Soviet Union. Both the Chilean and Grenadian revolutions were suppressed.[1] However, Cuba and Nicaragua survived as revolutionary examples in Latin America. In Asia, Kampuchea, Laos, reunified Vietnam and Afghanistan have undergone a complex series of revolutions. In the Middle East, South Yemen has been added to the revolutionary ranks. In Africa, Congo-Brazzaville, Somalia, Guinea-Bissau, Benin (formerly Dahomey), Mozambique, Cape Verde, Angola, Ethiopia and Eritrea provide a wide spectrum of revolutionary experience.

Revolutions in the fourth period overlap considerably in nature and in time (1959 onwards) with those of the third period. Fourth period revolutions combine the characteristics of national democracy and national liberation. Their leadership has been inspired by dialectical and historical materialism but contains a plurality of opinion and experience. Significantly, the Marxists leading these revolutions do not have as their immediate goal the establishment of a full socialist society. They argue that, in the countries of fourth-period revolutions, the objective and subjective conditions[2] are not yet conducive to the creation and consolidation of a classic socialist regime and economy. Nicaragua provides a prime example of this. Tomas Borge, Minister of the Interior and the only surviving founder of the Sandinistas is reported as having stated that:

Originally, the Sandinista Front had conceived of a different kind of revolution. In ideal terms it would be a deeply radical revolution, even at some point reaching the abolition of private property, a revolution within the classically socialist framework.

But reality taught us that, in the special conditions of Latin America and Nicaragua, this was not possible. [*Globe and Mail*, 7 September, 1985.]

He went on to note that the category of private ownership of the means of production would survive until a future generation decided otherwise.

These remarks gain additional interest since they follow on the analysis of Cuban President Fidel Castro that a new form of revolution was now needed. In contrast to Castro's expectations of the 1960s, socialist revolution was not on the agenda for Latin America in the 1980s:

> In Latin America, socialism is not the question. The Nicaraguans have not set socialism as an objective. Economic development and social reform are the question. No revolutionary movement—including the Salvadorans—has proposed socialism as an objective. . . . Their objective is national liberation. They have proposed a pluralistic system, economically and politically. [Castro interviewed by Torbjornsson, 1984, p. 17.]

Castro argued that to propose anything more than national liberation and social justice would be counter-revolutionary. To do so would be to invite the United States' intervention.

Evaluation of the Ghanaian Experience

While the statements of political leaders should always be subjected to thorough scrutiny, these particular analyses do seem to have considerable relevance to Ghana. The June Fourth Movement and the People's Revolutionary League of Ghana wanted to establish full socialism immediately. Their understanding of socialism was considerably influenced by the Soviet model. However, the June Fourth Movement was not able to successfully implement its revolutionary strategy. First, its 'quick-move-to-socialism' strategy did not conform to the national-democratic strategy of the charismatic leader of the December 31st revolution, J. J. Rawlings, and the New Democratic Movement. Lacking a leader capable of outshining Rawlings, the June Fourth Movement could have tried to use a developed political infrastructure of cadres as well as substantial economic aid from the Soviet bloc. The June Fourth Movement was unable to fulfill these alternatives. As June Fourth Movement leaders later acknowledged, the revolution was premature for them: they had a small number of inexperienced cadres deployed in some regions who were loosely organized in what was really a proto-movement rather than their intended Marxist–Leninist vanguard party. Moreover, they were unable to turn the defence committees into this party. Given time, they might have succeeded, but time they did not have. When June Fourth leaders visited the Soviet Union in mid-1982, the Soviet bloc failed to deliver sufficient financial assistance to solve Ghana's economic chaos. Consequently, the rest of the PNDC decided to turn elsewhere for economic aid and to follow a strategy that contained national democratic and NEP elements. This implied a reliance on the private sector. The June Fourth Movement interpreted this as a betrayal of the revolution and attempted an unsuccessful coup in October and November of 1982. Following this, they were dispersed by the rest of the PNDC.

Rawlings, the New Democratic Movement, the radical populists, the liberal patriots and others then bound themselves to a strategy that differed from the conventional national–democratic revolutionary phase in two important respects. First, unlike Cuba and China, there was little immediate prospect of establishing full socialism. There were too few socialists to rebuild the shattered economy. There was no widespread political base among the population at large from which the necessary support for socialism could be mobilized. In order to succeed in the primary task of economic reconstruction, therefore, support had to be gathered wherever it could be found. Consequently, if such a politically diverse group were to continue in this crucial role, then they would all expect to see aspects of their goals honoured and implemented by the revolution.

A second major divergence from the classic Soviet and national democratic models was that there was no tightly-knit communist party leading the revolution. A number of Marxist organizations played leading roles, but were restricted by the smallness of their numbers and by their inexperience from having an impact much beyond certain important posts in the senior levels of the administration, armed forces and political directorate.

The PNDC has been severely constrained by the economic and political conditions in Ghana. Accordingly, it is necessary to differentiate the PNDC's intentions from its ability to translate them into actuality. Coming to power at a time when the power of the Ghanaian state had largely collapsed (Chazan, 1983), the PNDC has faced the problem not only of trying to create new revolutionary centres of power such as the tribunals and defence committees but also of re-establishing the authority and legitimacy of the state of Ghana. The tendency in some quarters to blame all the limited number of cases of excesses on the PNDC ignores one central fact of the revolution and of Ghana: the legal hierarchy of authority had broken down. The revolution had to scramble to restore key elements of the old state—for example, to bring the soldiers and police under control—let alone create a new system of revolutionary authority. The lack of a central revolutionary party was crucial.

Unlike the Ethiopian revolution, the Ghanaian revolution has been mild. In Ethiopia there has been a systematic and large-scale use of bloodshed to 'advance' the revolution. By comparison, the Ghanaian revolution has been gentle and has respected human rights. There have been incidents, but on the whole they have occurred on the fringe as individual acts, not as government policy. Unlike Ethiopia, where political differences in the ruling Dergue were once settled by the members going for their guns and shooting each other, even PNDC members who attempted a coup were at worst imprisoned, later to be released into exile.[3]

The economic crisis and the limited human resources of the left combined to limit the implementation of the revolution's goals. The economic crisis has consumed much of the leadership's attention and energy. Many of the limited number of the revolutionary leadership have been devoted to managing this crisis and warding off attempts to overthrow the PNDC. Little energy was left over for detailed policy formulation and implementation in other areas. The shortage of cadres has meant that there has been little effective political supervision of the civil service, whose senior levels have been in large measure unsympathetic and whose junior levels have been demoralized by the inability of their salaries to meet the ravages of inflation. Consequently, the implementation of the revolution's policies has suffered.

The shortage of experienced political personnel has also affected the revolution's ability to conduct effective political education, socialization and recruitment. Until more are recruited and trained, the revolution will be hard pressed to develop the additional human resources necessary to consolidate the real, though limited, political, social and economic gains.

Foreign policy has focused on obtaining the necessary resources to implement economic strategy. Innovative proposals have been made in the area of social policy. However, the PNDC has argued that, until production is increased, the resources to turn these proposals into reality will be lacking. Thus, foreign and social policies have been of secondary importance to economic policy.

Whether the economic policy which includes the 'IMF heresy' will actually restore productivity and promote the end of poverty has been the subject of intense debate both within and without the PNDC. The massive influx of foreign capital has dramatically stopped the econ-omic rot at the macro-level. The productivity of the export sectors, which has benefited from this inflow, has once more proved to be the driving force of the economy (at least for the time being), just as it was in the 1940s and 1950s. Consumer goods have reappeared in street markets and their prices have been falling. Nevertheless, the scope of the necessary reconstruction of educational, health and other state social services is very considerable. Wages have fallen behind the price inflation of consumer goods. On the other hand, economic conditions for ordinary people have eased and considerable efforts have been made to address problems.

The challenge will be for the PNDC to see if it can use private business to promote growth at the micro- and macro-level, as well as facilitating social justice for the rest of society. At the very least, the December 31st revolution has provided new room for manœuvre, and experience in governing for those concerned with social justice. In addition, the PNDC has proved itself willing to take economic deci-sions that a number of previous governments had been unwilling to take. The PNDC has decided that until economic recovery has taken hold, social and political programmes will be put in abeyance. Rawlings, the IMF and the World Bank all see Ghana as the test case for West Africa. If the PNDC does not succeed, the future of Ghana is grim.

Notes

Chapter 1

1. For excellent discussions of the pitfalls of the concept of 'tribalism', see Molteno (1974) and Saul (1979a). For an analysis of ethnic conflict in Ghana and the way it has weakened governments and the national consciousness, see, for example, D. Brown (1982); AC (No. 9, 1977, p. 6–7), Aidoo (1983), Morrison (1983), Apronti (1978) and Chazan (1983).
2. For discussions of class and class consciousness in Ghana, see, for example, Aidoo (1983), Apronti (1978), C. K. Brown (1983), D. Brown (1982), Howard (1980), Morrison (1983), Ofori-Atta (1978), Sandbrook & Arn (1977, 1980), Gutkind (1979), Vercruijsse (1979).
3. See, for example, the work of Anquandah, Shinnie, Posnansky, Ozanne, Davies, Sutton, Lawrence, Kense, Effah-Gyamfi and Guvua, among others.
4. The Asante prefer their own spelling to Ashanti.
5. A full appreciation of the strengths and weaknesses of Nkrumah and those around him is not possible here. Card (1975) provides a most useful and perceptive brief evaluation. A sampling of the important literature would include Austin (1964), Apter (1968), Davidson (1973), Fitch & Oppenheimer (1966), the vitriol of T. Jones (1976) and Rathbone's elegance (1968, 1978). For one Soviet view, the reader might consult Smertin (1982).
6. For an analysis of the 1966–9 junta government, see, for example: Card (1975), Austin & Luckham (1975) and Pinkney (1972).
7. For the Busia period, see, for example, Card (1975) and Chazan (1983).
8. The best accounts of these years are those of Oquaye (1980) and Chazan (1983).
9. The most comprehensive account of the Limann period is Chazan (1983). For the AFRC period, see, for example, Okeke (1982) and Hansen and Collins (n.d.; 1980), Ninsin (1979).

Chapter 2

1. Mao argued that the Chinese revolution would be accomplished in two stages: a new democratic stage in which it was necessary for communists to ally with those elements of the bourgeoisie who were willing to fight imperialism, and even to allow the development of certain aspects of a 'capitalist economy', though only on the condition that socialist leadership in politics and the economy were ensured. Mao wrote extensively on this theme but two examples are, 'The Chinese Revolution and the Chinese Communist Party', 1939, pp. 305–34, particularly pp.320–1, 327, 329–30; and of course, 'On New Democracy', 1940, pp. 330–84, particularly pp. 348–50, 353 of Vol. 2 in *Selected Works of Mao Tse Tung*, Peking, Foreign Languages Press, 1965.
2. Kwame Nkrumah argued that all the countries and peoples of Africa should unite into a pan-African state in order to overcome poverty and foreign domination in the continent. See, for example, his *Africa Must Unite*.
3. The complexity of the problem has already been noted. Jeffries presents the controversial but interesting hypothesis that the major cause of the vast increase in administrative corruption, 'kalabule', trading, hyper-inflation and cocoa smuggling, which devastated the Ghanaian economy in 1975–79, lay in the economic policies of the Acheampong regime, and that these in turn followed logically from the attempt to maintain the orientation and structure of the economy [i.e. state intervention and attempted industrialization] as inherited from Nkrumah. Jeffries, July 1982, pp. 314–15.

Chapter 6

1. For a discussion of the conceptual differences between nationalist movements and national liberation movements which inadvertently parallels Duverger's 'cadre' or notable party and mass party, see Saul on FRELIMO (Saul & Arrighi, 1973).
2. Human settlement at Daboya has been identified as having existed for over three thousand years (interview with Peter Shinnie, Daboya, 22 July 1983; Kense, 1981; Guvua, 1985; Shinnie & Kense (forthcoming).
3. For details of allegations and convictions of corruption in the defence committees, see the daily newspapers, e.g. *People's Daily Graphic*, 25

August 1983. For Rawlings' self-criticism and other criticism of aspects of the defence committees, see his speech, 'Discipline and Productivity', 28 August 1983. Among other things, Rawlings criticized: (1) those members of the June Fourth Movement (formerly on the PNDC and NDC) who as university students and recent graduates had shown intellectual arrogance towards those who were not intellectuals and/or who did not agree with the June Fourth's strategy of a rapid move towards socialism and (2) those defence committee members who neglected economic production in order to attend political rallies and meetings.

4. For other evaluations of defence committees, see, for example, Adjei (1984), Amponsah (1983), Anin (1983), Kwasi (1984), Okine (1984) and Yeebo (1985).

Chapter 7

1. This estimate must be tentative given the circumstances surrounding such events. Accordingly, only those plots and attempts which were reported have been considered here. According to one confidential report, the Ghana Democratic Movement claimed that five plots in November and December 1984 were discovered by the PNDC. This same source had earlier claimed that a Cuban brigade was in Ghana. This was incorrect.

2. I would like to thank Professor P. L. Shinnie and Mrs A. Shinnie for their assistance in drawing up a provisional ethno-linguistic affiliation for those thought to be involved in the various attempted coups and plots.

Chapter 8

1. For a similar case, see Canada's province of Alberta which attempted to break out of its dependence on oil by advocating first industrialization, then diversification, and now free trade with the United States (Pratt, 1977).

2. To the outsider, the range of Nkrumah's accomplishments seem astounding. During July and August of 1984, a group of university students from Burkina Faso were touring Ghana as part of the fraternal agreements between the two revolutions. They told me that they

admired Ghana for its infrastructure, much of which was built under Nkrumah's administration. Again and again when inquiring as to the date of construction of different facilities in Daboya and other part of the north, I was told that they had been begun or build during Nkrumah's time (see Ray, Kense and Guvua). See also Gore (1984), Jeffries (1982), and Killick (1983).

3. For a listing of foreign aid from multilateral and bilteral sources, see *People's Daily Graphic*, 24 December 1984, p. 3.

4. By mid-1985, two kilograms (one bowl) of rice sold for Cedis 110 in government stores but only Cedis 80 in the market (personal communication, 20 August 1985).

5. *Africa Confidential* has argued that there are parallels between the foreign investment portions of the PNDC's economic recovery programme and Limann's investment code (*AC*, **25**, No. 12, 6 June 1984, p. 4) which was denounced by Rawlings and the other revolutionaries. At a meeting of a partial 'mini-cabinet', I observed that foreign investment was being encouraged if it produced new capital and expertise in amounts sufficient to appreciably increase key exports. Rawlings, when asked whether a certain timber entrepreneur would be welcomed back to Ghana, replied, 'Ah yes, I remember him from 1979—when he pays Ghana the twenty million Cedis he owes us [for back taxes] he will be welcome back, but not until then.' (August 1984).

6. For the December 31st revolutionary period, see, for example, Konings (1984a, 1984b).

7. For a selection of literature on the pre-31 December 1981 labour movement in Ghana, see, for example, Cowan (1960), Davis (1966), Debrah (1984), Fitch & Oppenheimer (1966), Gray (1977, 1980, 1981), Jeffries (1978), Kraus (1978), Silver (1978) and Trachtman (1961).

8. This section is primarily based on a series of interviews, many of which cannot be attributed at the present time. Those that can be acknowledged include a series conducted in Accra: Rawlings, 7, 8 August 1984; Annan (PNDC member), 3 August 1984; Tsikata (PNDC member), July 1984; Obeng (PNDC Co-ordinating Secretary), August 1984; Botchwey (Finance Secretary), July 1984; Yahaya (Northern Regional Secretary), Tamale, June–August 1983, 1984; Ndebugre (Upper East and later Agriculture Secretary), Bolgatanga, 27 June 1983. Other sources included the *Ghanaian Times* (Accra), the *People's Daily Graphic* (Accra), *Ghana Newsletter* (Netherlands), *Africa Confidential*, (London), *West Africa*, (London), Pagni (1985) and Kraus (1982, 1983, 1985).

9. See, for example, Austin (1975), Bening (1976), Bibby and Peil (1974), Debrah (1985), J. Kaufert (1980), P. Kauffert (1976), McKown & Finlay (1976), Peil (1973), Smart (1975), Southall & J. Kaufert (1974).
10. See, for example, Date-Bah (1984), Dumor (1983), Harrell-Bond & Fraker (1980), Mikell (1983), Okala & Mabey (1975) and Okali (1979).

Chapter 9

1. Chile has been added to Szajkowski's list. The Chile of the Popular Unity government reflected the Euro-communist model more than the national liberation model. Also, Allende ignored Marx's comments on the Paris Commune of 1871 with regard to taking over the 'old' state.
2. Marxism is still only a new-born force. As an intellectual and social movement it is less than 150 years old. As a government, the oldest case is the Soviet Union, which was created in 1917—not even seventy years ago. In historical terms this young movement is still weak, outside the Soviet Union. It is not surprising, therefore, to discover that Marxist movements often find themselves adapting away from the Soviet model to reflect the local situation more closely. Certainly this has been the case in Ghana.
3. Another was executed for the murder of three judges and a retired army officer.

Select Bibliography

Ablorh–Objidja, E., 1982. 'Ghana: The Revolution That Never Was', *Crisis*, **89**, (1), pp. 22–5.

Abugri, Charles, 1983. 'The Economic Recovery Dilemma of Ghana', *Ghana Newsletter*, No. 5, August.

Ada, Sam, 1982. 'Ghana Confronts 25 Years of Economic Confusion: Jerry Rawlings' New Government Needs More Than Revolutionary Fervour To Overcome Ghana's Problems', *South*, June, pp. 18–21.

Addo, Max, 1978. *Ghana's Foreign Policy in Retrospect*. Accra, Waterville Publishing House.

Adjei, Francis, April 1984. 'Power to the People: A Study of the Defence Committees Since December 31st Revolution in Ghana', B.A. long essay, Political Science, University of Ghana, Legon.

Africa, 1979. 'Ghana: The Self-limiting Revolution', August, pp. 14–17.

—— 1980a. 'Which Way Ghana?' (interview with President Hilla Limann), March, pp. 16–23.

—— 1980b. 'Ghana: Special Study (Economic and Political Conditions)', March, pp. 39–62.

Africa Report, 1982. 'Ghana's "Holy War"', *Africa Report*, May–June (27), pp. 12–15.

Agyeman-Badu, Yaw, & Osei-Hwedie, Kwaku, 1982. *The Political Economy of Instability: Colonial Legacy, Inequality and Political Instability in Ghana*. Lawrenceville (Virginia), Brunswick.

Ahiakpor, J. C. W., 1985. 'The Success and Failure of Dependency Theory: The Experience of Ghana', *International Organization*, 39, No. 3 (Summer).

Aidoo, Thomas Akwasi, 1983. 'Ghana: Social Class, the December Coup (1981), and the Prospects for Socialism, *Contemporary Marxism*, Spring, pp. 142–59.

Ajayi, J. F. A., & Crowder, Michael, (eds), 1974, 1976. *History of West Africa*, Vol. 1, 2nd edn (1976), Vol. 2 (1974), Harlow, Essex, Longman.

Amnesty International, 1975–1984. *International Report*. London, Amnesty International.

—— , 1983. 'Amnesty International's Concerns in the Republic of Ghana', London, Amnesty International Background Paper, July.

—— , 1984a. *Torture in the Eighties*. London, Amnesty International Publications.

—— , 1984b. 'The Public Tribunals in Ghana', London, Amnesty International, AI Index: AFR-28/10/84, July.

—— , 1984c. 'Ghana: The Summary Execution or Detention Without Trial of People Suspected of Attempting to Overthrow the Government', London, Amnesty International, AI Index AFR-28/14/84, August.

Amoako-Tuffour, Joe, 1985. 'Bureaucratic Corruption and Persistent Inefficiency in Ghana: An Economic Analysis', Paper presented to the South-South Conference (CAAS-CALACS), Montreal, 15–17 May.

Amonoo, Benjamin, 1981. *Ghana 1957–: The Politics of Institutional Dualism.* London, Allen & Unwin.

Amponsah, Nicholas, April 1983. 'The Impact of the December 31 Revolution on the Rural Ghana—The Case of Nkoranza in the Brong Ahafo Region of Ghana', B.A. long essay, Political Science, University of Ghana, Legon.

Andrae, Gunilla, 1981. *Industry in Ghana: Production Form and Spatial Structure.* Sweden, Scandinavian Institute of African Studies.

Anin, Kobina F. G., May 1983. '31st December: A Revolution or a Mere Change in the Dramatis Personae?', B.A. long essay, Political Science, University of Ghana, Legon.

Ankama, Silvester Kwadio, 1983. *Police History: Some Aspects in England and Ghana.* Ilford, Essex, Silkan Books.

Anquandah, James, 1982a. 'The Archaeological Evidence for the Emergence of Akan Civilisation', *Tarikh*, **7** (2), pp. 9–21.

—— , 1982b. *Rediscovering Ghana's Past.* London, Longman Group.

Anthony, Earl, 1971. 'Pan-African Socialism', *Black Scholar*, **3** (2), pp. 40–5.

Apronti, James, 1978. 'Culture Without Chiefs: An Essay Against The Concept of "Natural" Rulers', *Studia Africana*, **1** (2), pp. 118–26.

Apter, David, 1968. *Ghana in Transition*, rev. edn. New York, Atheneum.

Arhin, Kwame, 1967. 'The Structure of Greater Ashanti', *Journal of African History*, **8** (1).

—— (forthcoming) *Chieftancy in Ghana*, Accra.

Assimeng, Max, 1981. *Social Structure of Ghana: a Study in Persistence and Change.* Accra-Tema, Ghana Publishing Corporation.

Austin, Dennis, 1964. *Politics in Ghana 1946–60.* London, Oxford University Press.

—— , 1975. 'State and University in Ghana', *Round Table*.

—— , & Luckham, Robin (eds), 1975. *Politicians and Soldiers in Ghana 1966–1972*, London, Frank Cass.

Ayrton, Peter (ed.), 1982. *World View 1983: an Economic and Geopolitical Yearbook.* London, Pluto Press (Paris, Maspero).

164   *Select Bibliography*

Barrows, Walter L., 1974. 'Comparative Grassroots Politics in Africa', *World Politics*, **26** (2), pp. 283–97.

Bawuah, Kwadwo, 1980. 'Some Aspects of Political-Economy of Development: The Case of Ghana 1950–1966', Ph.D. thesis, Blacksburg, Virginia, Polytechnic Institute and State University.

Baynham, S. J., 1976. 'The military in Ghanaian politics', *Army Quarterly and Defence Journal*, **106** (4), pp. 428–39.

Bening, R. B., 1976. 'Colonial Control and the Provision of Education in Northern Ghana, 1908–1951', *Universitas*, University of Ghana, Dept. of Philosophy, **5** (2), May–November, pp. 58–99.

Bibby, John, & Peil, Margaret, 1974. 'Research Notes: Secondary Education in Ghana: Private Enterprise and Social Selection', *Sociology of Education*, **47** (3), pp. 399–418.

Birmingham, Walter; Neustadt, I., & Omaboe, E. N. (eds), 1966/67. *A Study of Contemporary Ghana, Vol. 1: The Economy of Ghana: Vol. 2: Some Aspects of Social Structure*. London, Allen & Unwin.

Bluwey, Gilbert K., 1976. 'Continuity and Change in Ghana's Foreign Policy in the Post-Nkrumah Era (1966–1975)', Ph.D. dissertation, Howard University.

Boahen, Adu, 1966. 'The Origins of the Akan', *Ghana Notes and Queries*, **9**, pp. 3–10.

—— , 1974. 'Politics of Ghana, 1800–1874', in *History of West Africa*, J. F. A. Ajayi and M. Crowder (eds), Harlow, Essex, Longman.

Braimah, J. A., 1967. *The Two Isanwurfos*. London, Longman.

Brittan, Victoria, 1983. 'Ghana's Precarious Revolution', *New Left Review*, July/August, pp. 50–61.

Brown, C. K., 1978. 'The Ghanaian Rural Youth: Resource for Social Development', *Ghana Social Science Journal*, **5** (1), pp. 26–46.

—— , 1983. 'Social Structure and Rural Poverty in Ghana', *Rural Africana*, **17**, pp. 19–29.

Brown, David, 1979. 'Ghana: From Protest to Participation', *Contemporary Review* (Britain), **234**, (1360), pp. 237–44.

—— , 1982. 'Who Are the Tribalists? Social Pluralism and Political Ideology in Ghana', *African Affairs*, **322** (January), pp. 37–69.

Bryce, T. E., 1972. 'A Rural Nutrition Clinic in Ghana', *Canadian Journal of Public Health*, **63** (6), pp. 530–31.

Burnett, Nicholas, 1980. 'Kaiser Shortcircuits Ghanaian Development', *Multinational Monitor*, **1** (Fall), pp. 6–9.

Cabral, Amilcar, 1969. *Revolution in Guinea: selected texts by Amilcar Cabral*, R. Handyside (ed. and trans.). New York and London, Monthly Review Press.

—— , 1977/78. 'The Role of Culture in the Struggle for Independence', *International Journal of Politics*, **7** (4), pp. 18–43.

—— , 1980. *Unity and Struggle*, Michael Wolfers (ed. and trans.). London, Heinemann.

Canadian International Development Agency (CIDA), 1985. *A Developing World*. Hull, Quebec.

Card, Emily, 1975. 'The Political Economy of Ghana', in *The Political Economy of Africa* R. Harris (ed.). New York, John Wiley.

Carr, Edward Hallett, 1952. *The Bolshevik Revolution 1917-1923*, 3 vols. in *A History of Soviet Russia*, reprinted 1983. Harmondsworth, Penguin.

Case, Glenna, 1979. 'Wasipe under the Ngbanya: Polity, Economy and Society in Northern Ghana (Volumes I and II)', Ph.D. dissertation, Northwestern University.

Chazan, Naomi, 1978. 'Ghanaian Political Studies in Transition: a Reflection on Some Recent Contributions', *Development and Change*, Netherlands, **9** (3), pp. 479–503.

Chazan, Naomi, 1983. *An Anatomy of Ghanaian Politics: Managing Political Recession, 1969-1982*. Boulder, Colorado, Westview Press.

Checole, Kassahun, 1982. 'Jerry Rawlings' Second Coup in Ghana: A Response to "Exploitation ... Greed and Corruption," and the IMF (International Monetary Fund)', *Multinational Monitor* **3** (February), pp. 11–13.

Chick, John D., 1976. '*The Ashanti Times*: A Footnote to Ghanaian Press History', *African Affairs* (Britain), **76** (302), pp. 80–94.

Cohen, D. L., & Tribe, M. A., 1972. 'Suppliers' Credits in Ghana and Uganda: An Aspect of the Imperialist System', *Journal of Modern African Studies* (Britain), **19** (4), pp. 525–41.

Cohen, Robert, 1980. 'Resistance and Hidden forms of Consciousness Amongst African Workers', *Review of African Political Economy*, **19** (September/December), pp. 8–22.

Communist Party of the Soviet Union (CPSU), O. V. Kuusinen *et al.*, 1963. *Fundamentals of Marxism-Leninism Manual*. Moscow, Foreign Languages Publishing House, 2nd rev. edn.

Contee, Clarence G., 1971. 'A critical friendship begins: DuBois and Nkrumah: 1935-1945', *Crisis*, **78** (6), pp. 181–5.

Cowan, E. A., 1960. *Evolution of Trade Unionism in Ghana*. Accra, TUC.

Darkoh, Michael, B. K., 1973. 'Manufacturing in Ghana, 1957-1967', *Bulletin de l'Institut Fondamental d'Afrique Noire, Série B* (Senegal), **35** (4), pp. 813–53.

—— , 1976. 'An Outline of post-1966 Regional Planning and Rural Development in Ghana', *Pan-African Journal* (Kenya) **9** (2), pp. 153–67.

Date-Bah, Eugenia, 1984. 'Rural women, their activities and technology in Ghana: an overview' in *Rural Women and Development*, Geneva, ILO (International Labour Organization).

Davidson, Basil, 1973. *Black Star: A View of the Life of Kwame Nkrumah*. London, Penguin.

—— 1974, *Growing from Grass Roots*. London, Committee for Freedom in Mozambique, Angola and Guinea.

Davies, Ioan, 1966. *African Trade Unions*. Harmondsworth, Penguin.

Davies, Oliver, 1967. *West Africa Before the Europeans*. London, Methuen.

Debelian, Levon, 1972. 'The Volta River Resettlement Program', *Land Reform, Land Settlement and Cooperatives*, vol. 1, pp. 18–35.

Debrah, Yaw, 1984. 'Some Aspects of the Sociology of Work in Ghana', Antigonish, Canadian Association of African Studies.

—— , 1985. 'Teacher Professionalization in Ghana', Montreal, Canadian Association of African Studies, May, pp. 15–17.

Decalo, Samuel, 1973. 'Military Coups and Military Regimes in Africa', *Journal of Modern African Studies* (Britain), **11** (1), pp. 105–27.

Degenhardt, Henry W., 1983. *Political Dissent—An International Guide to Dissident, Extra-Parliamentary Guerrilla and Illegal Political Movements*. London, Longman.

Dickson, K. B., 1969. *A Historical Geography of Ghana*. Cambridge, Cambridge University Press.

Dolphyne, Florence Abena, 1982. 'Akan Language Patterns and Development', *Tarikh*, **7** (2), pp. 35–45.

Downey, J. A., 1981. 'The History and Functions of Some Ghanaian Organizations Represented in the IDS Library', *African Research and Documentation* (Britain), **25**, pp. 13–24.

Dumor, Ernest, 1976. 'Indigenous Farming Systems and Implications for Rural Youth Programs in Ghana', *Rural Africana*, **30** (Spring), pp. 31–40.

—— 1983. 'Women in Rural Development in Ghana', *Rural Africana*, **17** (Fall), pp. 69–81.

Dunn, John (ed.), 1978. *West African States: Failure and Promise: A Study in Comparative Politics*. Cambridge, Cambridge University Press.

Duverger, Maurice, 1964. *Political Parties*, rev. edn. London, Methuen.

Effah-Gyamfi, Kwaku, 1985. *Bono Manso: An Archaeological Investigation into Early Akan Urbanism*. Calgary, University of Calgary Press, African Occasional Papers No. 2.

Eisenstadt, S. N., 1981. 'Cultural Traditions and Political Dynamics: The Origins and Modes of Ideological Politics', *British Journal of Sociology*, **32** (2), pp. 155–81.

Ekwelieh, Sylvanus, A., 1978. 'The genesis of press control in Ghana', *Gazette*, **24**, (3), pp. 196–206.

Elliot, Charles, 1975. *Patterns of Poverty in the Third World: A Study of Social and Economic Stratification*. New York, Praeger.

Eluwa, G. I. C., 1974. 'Casely Hayford and African Emancipation', *Pan-African Journal* (Kenya), **7** (2), pp. 111–18.

Fage, J. D. (ed.), 1959. 'A New Check List of the Forts and Castles of Ghana', *Transactions of the Historical Society of Ghana*, **4** (1), pp. 57–67.

—— , & Verity, Maureen, 1978. *An Atlas of African History*, 2nd edn. London, Edward Arnold.

Fanon, Frantz, 1963. *The Wretched of the Earth*. New York, Grove Press.

Ferguson, Phyllis, 1973. 'Islamization in Dagbon: A Study of the Alfanema of Yendi', Ph.D. thesis, University of Cambridge.

Fitch, Bob, & Oppenheimer, Mary, 1966. *Ghana: End of an Illusion*. New York, Monthly Review Press.

Folson, B. G. D., 1977. 'The Marxist Period in the Development of Socialist Ideology in Ghana', *Universitas* (Ghana), **6** (1), pp. 3–23.

Forde, D., & Kaberry, P. M., (eds) 1967. *West African Kingdoms in the Nineteenth Century*. London, Oxford University Press.

Fynn, John Kofi, 1971. *Asante and Its Neighbours 1700–1807*. Harlow, Essex, Longman.

—— , (guest ed.), 1982a. 'Akan History and Culture', *Tarikh*, **7** (2).

—— , 1982b. 'Introduction [to Akan History and Culture]', in *Tarikh*, **7** (2), pp. 1–7.

—— , 1982c. 'Trade and Politics in Akanland', *Tarikh*, **7** (2), pp. 23–34.

Gariba, Sulley, 1985. 'CIDA, the State, and Rural Development in the Northern Region of Ghana', Paper presented to the South-South Conference (CAAS and CALACS) Montreal, 15–17 May.

Gavua, Kodzo, 1985. 'Daboya and the Kintampo Culture of Ghana', M.A. thesis, University of Calgary.

Ghana, Census Office, 1964. *1960 Population Census of Ghana Special Report 'E'*, *Tribes of Ghana*, Accra.

Ghana Information Service, 1981. 'Spotlight on Ghana', *West Africa*, 11 May, pp. 1035–42.

Godelier, Maurice, 1971. 'Myth and History', *New Left Review*, **69**, pp. 93–112.

Goody, J., 1966. 'Circulating Succession Among the Gonja' in J. Goody (ed.), *Succession to High Office*, Cambridge, Cambridge University Press.

—— , 1967. 'The Over-Kingdom of Gonja' in *West African Kingdoms in the*

Nineteenth Century, D. Forde & P. Kaberry (eds), London, Oxford University Press.

—, 1971. *Technology, Tradition, and the State in Africa*. London, Oxford University Press.

Gore, Louise, 1984. 'The Rawlings Regimes in Ghana 1979–1983: The Political Economy of Military Intervention', Kingston, Canada, Studies in National and International Development, Occasional Papers No. 84–102, Queen's University.

Gray, Paul S., 1977. 'The Institutionalization of Organized Labour in Ghana', Ph.D. dissertation, Yale University.

—, 1980. 'Collective Bargaining in Ghana', *Industrial Relations*, **19** (Spring), pp. 179–91.

—, 1981. 'The Genesis of Trade Unions in Ghana', *Journal of African Studies*, **8** (Summer), pp. 72–8.

—, 1981. *Unions and Leaders in Ghana: A Model of Development*. Buffalo, Conch Magazine Ltd.

Greene, S. A., 1981. 'The Anlo-Ewe: Their Economy, Society and External Relations in the Eighteenth Century', Ph.D., Northwestern University.

Gutkind, Peter, 1979. Review of R. Sandbrook and J. Arn, 'The Labouring Poor and Urban Class Formation: The Case of Greater Accra' (Montreal, 1977), reviewed in *The International Journal of African Historical Studies*, **12** (1), pp. 83–95.

Haight, B., 1981. 'Bole and Gonja, Contributions to the History of Northern Ghana', 3 vols. Ph.D. Northwestern University.

Halliday, Fred, 1980. 'War and Revolution in Afghanistan', *New Left Review*, **119** (January–February), pp. 20–41.

Hansen, Emanuel, 1984. 'Review: Politicians, Politics and Policies in Ghana', *Journal of African Marxists*, **6** (October), pp. 118–26.

—, & Collins, Paul, 1980. 'The Army, The State and The "Rawlings Revolution" in Ghana', *African Affairs*, **79** (314), pp. 3–23.

Harkness, Rose Mae, 1984. 'Dependency, Patriarchy and Participation: An Analysis by Gender of Development in the Upper Region of Ghana', Paper delivered to the Annual Meeting of the Canadian Association of African Studies, Antigonish, 9–12 May 1984.

Harrell-Bond, Barbara E., 1979. 'Ghana's Troubled Transition to Civilian Government', *American University Field Staff Reports*, No. 48.

—, 1980a. 'Diary of a Revolution "Which Might Have Been": pt. 1, "Power was Virtually Lying on the Floor", *American University Field Staff Reports*, No. 24.

—, 1980b. 'Diary of a Revolution "Which Might Have Been": pt. 2, "To Cut a Real Revolution Right in the Middle'", *American University Field Staff Reports*, No. 25.

—— , & Fraker, Anne, 1980. 'Women and the 1979 Ghana Revolution', *American University Field Staff Reports*, No. 4.

Harris, D. J., 1982. 'The Recent Political Upheavals in Ghana', *World Today*, (London), **36** (January), pp. 225–32.

Harris, Janette Hoston, 1972. 'Ghana: The Forging of a Nation', *Negro History Bulletin*, **35** (4), pp. 89–91.

Hecht, Robert, 1978. 'The Rise of Radical African studies', *Journal of Development Studies* (Britain), **15** (1), pp. 120–6.

Heh, Benjamin Kwadzo, 1983. 'The 31st December Event in Ghana: a Study of the Fall of Ghana's Third Republic', B.A. long essay, Political Science, University of Ghana, Legon.

Henriksen, Thomas H. (ed.), 1981. *Communist Powers and Sub-Saharan Africa*. Stanford, Hoover Institution Press.

Hettne, Bjorn, 1980. 'Soldiers and Politics', *Journal of Peace Research*, **17** (2), pp. 173–93.

Hewlett, Sylvia Ann, 1979. 'Human Rights and Economic Realities: Trade-offs in Historical Perspective', *Political Science Quarterly*, **94** (3), pp. 453–73.

Hinderink, J., & Sterkenburg, J. J., 1982. 'The Aims, the Methods, and the Means: Agricultural Production Performance and Agricultural Policy in Selected African Countries', Diskussiestukken No. 16, Vakgroep Sociale Geografie van Ontwikkelingslander, Geografisch Institute, Rijksuniversiteit, Utrecht.

Hodgkin, Thomas Lionel, 1957. *Nationalism in Colonial Africa*. New York, New York University Press.

Hopkins, A. (Tony) G., 1973. *An Economic History of West Africa*. London, Longman.

Howard, Rhoda, 1980. 'Formation and Stratification of the Peasantry in Colonial Ghana', *Journal of Peasant Studies* (London), **8** (11), pp. 61–80.

Hutchful, Eboe, 1979. 'Organizational Instability in African Military Forces: The Case of the Ghanaian Army', *International Society Science Journal* (France) **31** (4), pp. 606–18.

Huntington, Samuel, 1968. *Political Order in Changing Societies*. New Haven, Yale University Press.

Ibingiva, Grace Stuart, 1980. *African Upheavals Since Independence*. Boulder, Colorado, Westview.

Ingham, Barbara, 1979. 'Vent for Surplus Reconsidered with Ghanaian Evidence', *Journal of Development Studies* (Britain), **15** (3), pp. 19–37.

International Currency Review, 1979. 'The Causes of Hyperinflation in Ghana', **11** (3), pp. 41–6.

International Institute for Strategic Studies, 1985. *The Military Balance 1985–1986*. London, International Institute for Strategic Studies.

Ismael, Tareq Y., 1976. *The Arab Left*. Syracuse, Syracuse University Press.

James, C. L. R., 1977. *Nkrumah and the Ghana Revolution*. London, Allison and Busby (1982 Preface).

Janke, Peter, 1978. 'Marxist Statecraft in Africa: What Future?', *Conflict Studies*, No. 95 (May).

Janowitz, Morris, 1964. *The Military in the Political Development of New Nations: an Essay in Comparative Analysis*. Chicago, University of Chicago Press.

Jeffries, Richard, 1978. *Class, Power and Ideology in Ghana: The Railway of Sekondi*, Cambridge, Cambridge University Press.

— 1980. 'The Ghanaian elections of 1979', *African Affairs*, **316** (July), pp. 397–414.

— , 1982. 'Rawlings and the Political Economy of Underdevelopment in Ghana', *African Affairs*, **324** (July), pp. 307–17.

Jones, D. H., 1962. 'Jakpa and The Foundations of Gonja', *Transactions of The Historical Society of Ghana*, **6**, pp. 1–29.

Jones, Trevor, 1976. *Ghana's First Republic 1960–1966: the Pursuit of the Political Kingdom*. London, Methuen.

Kaplan, Irving; McLaughlin, James L.; Marvin, Barbara, J.; Moeller, Philip W.; Nelson, Harold D., & Whitaker, Donald P., 1971. *Area Handbook for Ghana*. Washington, Foreign Area Studies, The American University and US Government Printing Office.

Kaufert, Joseph M., 1980. 'Situational Ethnic Identity in Ghana: A Survey of University Students', in *Values, Identity and National Integration: Empirical Research in Africa*, John Paden (ed.), Evanston, Northwestern University Press, pp. 53–74.

Kauffert, Patricia Leyland, 1976. 'Christianity, Education and Politics in a Ghanaian Community', *West African Journal of Sociology and Political Science*, **1** (2), pp. 133–46.

Kennedy, Paul, 1977. 'African businessmen and foreign capital: collaboration or conflict', *African Affairs* (Britain), **76** (303), pp. 177–94.

Kense, François J., 1981. 'Daboya: a Gonja Frontier', Ph.D. thesis, University of Calgary.

Kidron, Michael, & Smith, Dan, 1983. *The War Atlas: Armed Conflict–Armed Peace*. London, Pan.

Killick, Tony, 1983. 'The role of the Public Sector in the Industrialization of African Developing Countries', *Industry and Development*, (7), pp. 57–88.

Kimble, David, 1963. *A Political History of Ghana 1850-1928*. London, Oxford University Press.

Kinzer, Stephen, 1985. 'Charismatic Master Fights for Nicaragua', *Globe and Mail* (Toronto), *New York Times* Service, 7 September, p. 9.

Kirk-Greene, A. H. M., 1981. *'Stay By Your Radios': Documentation for a Study of Military Government in Tropical Africa*. African Social Research Documents, Vol. 12. Leiden, Afrika-Studiecentrum and Cambridge, African Studies Centre.

Kofi, Tetteh, A., 1975. 'Toward the "Abibirim" Strategy of Development: a Formal Articulation', *Universitas* (Ghana), **5** (1), pp. 42–67.

Konings, Piet, 1984a. 'Workers and Workers' Defence Committees in Ghanaian Revolution—Part One: The Workers' Defence Committees', *Ghana Newsletter*, May, pp. 4–10.

— 1984b, 'Workers and Workers Movement in Ghananian Revolution—Part Two: The Trade Unions', *Ghana Newletter*, Summer, pp. 14–21.

Kooperman, Leonard, & Rosenberg, Stephen, 1977. 'The British Administrative Legacy in Kenya and Ghana', *International Review of Administrative Sciences*, **43** (3), pp. 267–72.

Kraus, Jon, 1978. 'Extent and Character of Collective Worker Protest, 1945–51', Fredonia, Department of Political Science, State University of New York.

— 1980. 'The Political Economy of Conflict in Ghana', *Africa Report*, **25** (March/April), pp. 9–16.

— , 1982. 'Rawlings' Second Coming', *Africa Report*, **27** (March/April) (2), pp. 59–66.

— , 1983. 'Revolution and the Military in Ghana', *Current History*, **82** (March), pp. 115–19.

— , 1985. 'Ghana's Radical Populist Regime', *Current History*, April, pp. 164–8, 186–7.

Kristof, Nicholas D., 1982. 'Ghana's Economy Sinks into Quagmire as Rawlings Temporizes on Solutions', *Wall Street Journal*, **199**, 26 April, p. 31.

Kronholz, June, 1982. 'Dark Continent: Ghana's Economic Skid Illustrates Bleak Spiral of Poverty in Africa', *Wall Street Journal*, **199**, 4 January, p. 1.

Kuan, Chung, 1977. 'A Case Study of Chinese Communist Subversive Activity in Africa: Relations Between Red China and Ghana (1964–1966)', Taipei, Taiwan, World Anti-Communist League (Taiwan), China Chapter Asian Peoples' Anti-Communist League.

Kwamena-Poh, M. A., 1973. *Government and Politics in the Akuapem State 1730–1850*. Harlow, Essex, Longman.

Kwasi, Hayford Benjamin K., 1984. 'Defence Committees as Organs for the Social and Political Transformation of Ghana', B.A. long essay, Political Science, University of Ghana, Legon.

Lacina, Karel, 1978. 'The Role of the Army in the Political Life of Contemporary Africa', *Ceskoslovensky Casopis Hist*. (Czechoslovakia), **26** (6), pp. 801–20.

Lenin, V. I., 1957. *The National-Liberational Movement in the East*. Moscow, Foreign Languages Publishing House.

——— , 1962. *On Britain*. Moscow, Foreign Languages Publishing House.

Levtzion, Nehemia, 1968. *Muslims and Chiefs in West Africa*. Oxford, Clarendon Press.

Lewycky, Dennis and White, Susan, 1979. *An African Abstract: A Brief Background to Issues and Events*. Winnipeg, Manitoba Council for International Cooperation.

Libby, Ronald T., 1976. 'External Co-optation of a Less Developed Country's Policy Making: The Case of Ghana, 1969–1972', *World Politics*, **29** (1), pp. 67–89.

Lipton, Michael, 1971. *Why Poor People Stay Poor: A Study of Urban Bias in World Development*. London, Temple Smith.

Matata, Godwin, 1982. 'Ghana', *Africa*, February, pp. 12–17.

May, Clifford D., 1984. 'Newly Stable Ghana Begins Showing Signs of Prosperity', *New York Times*, 11 November 1984.

McCain, James A., 1979. 'Attitudes Towards Socialism, Policy and Leadership in Ghana', *African Studies Review*, **22** (1), pp. 149–69.

McCarthy, D. M. P., 1975. 'Comments [on Reynold's Economic Imperialism: The Case of the Gold Coast, 94–116]', *Journal of Economic History*, **35** (1), pp. 134–7.

McKown, R. E., & Finlay, David J., 1976. 'Ghana's Status System: Reflections on University and Society', *Journal of Asian and African Studies*, **11**, Nos. 3–4, pp. 166–79.

Mikell, Gwendolyn, 1983. 'African Women Within Nations in Crisis', *TransAfrica Forum*, **2** (Summer), pp. 21–33.

Molteno, Robert, 1974. 'Cleavage and Conflict in Zambian Politics: a Study in Sectionalism', in *Politics in Zambia* (ed.), William Tordoff, Berkeley and Los Angeles, University of California Press, pp. 62–106.

Mondlane, Eduardo, 1969. *The Struggle for Mozambique*. Harmondsworth, Penguin Books.

Morrison, Minion K. C., 1983. 'Ethnicity and Integration: Dynamics of Change and Resilience in Contemporary Ghana', *Comparative Political Studies*, **15** (4), pp. 445–68.

Mufson, Stephen, 1983. 'End of a Dream: Once the Showpiece of Black Africa, Ghana is Now Near Collapse', *Wall Street Journal*, **201**, 28 March, p. 1.

Nelles, H. V., 1974. *The Politics of Development: Forests, Mines and Hydro-Electric Power in Ontario, 1849-1941*. Toronto, Macmillan.

New African Development, 1977. 'Ghana's 20 Years' (London), **11** (March), pp. 184–90.

Ninsin, Kwame, (forthcoming), 'Social and Political Pressures on Land Rights in Ghana,' in C. K. Brown and A. Thakur (eds.), *Rural Sociology of West Africa.*

Nkemdirim, Bernard A., 1977. 'Reflections on Political Conflict, Rebellion, and Revolution in Africa', *Journal of Modern African Studies*, **15** (1), pp. 75–90.

Nketia, J. H., Kwabena, 1982. 'The Musical Traditions of the Akan', *Tarikh*, **7** (2), pp. 47–59.

Nkrumah, Kwame, 1957. *Ghana: an Autobiography*. London, Nelson.

—— , 1965. *Necolonialism: the Last Stage of Imperialism*. New York, International Publishers.

North, Liisa, 1982. *Bitter Grounds: Roots of Revolt in El Salvador*. Toronto, Between the Lines.

Novicki, Margaret A., 1984a. 'Flt. Lt. Jerry Rawlings, Chairman of the Provisional National Defence Council, Ghana', *Africa Report*, **29** (2) (March–April), pp. 4–8.

—— , 1984b. 'The Economics of the Rawlings Revolution', *Africa Report*, September/October, pp. 42–7.

Odetola, T. Olatunde, 1982. *Military Regimes and Development: A Comparative Analysis of African States*. London, Allen & Unwin.

Odotei, I., 1972. 'The Ga and Their Neighbours', Ph.D. thesis, University of Ghana.

Ofori-Atta, J. 1978, 'Income Redistribution in Ghana: A Study of Rural Development', *Ghana Social Science Journal*, **5** (1), May, pp. 1–25.

Ogbu, J. U., 1973. 'Seasonal Hunger in Tropical Africa as a Cultural Phenomenon', *Africa*, **43** (4), pp. 317–32.

Okala, C. & Mabey, S., 1975. 'Women in Agriculture in Southern Ghana', *Manpower and Unemployment Research in Africa*, **8** (2), pp. 13–40.

Okali, C., 1979. 'The Changing Economic Position of Women in Rural Communities in West Africa', *Africana Marburgensia*, **12** (1/2), pp. 59–63.

Okeke, Barbara E., 1982. *4 June: A Revolution Betrayed*. Enugu, Nigeria, Ikenga Publishers.

Okine, Isaac T., 1984. 'One Year in Office of the PNDC: A General Assessment', B.A. long essay, Political Science, University of Ghana, Legon.

Opoku, Kofi Asare, 1982. 'The World View of the Akan', *Tarikh*, 7 (2), pp. 61–73.

Oquaye, Mike, 1980. *Politics in Ghana, 1972–79*. Accra, Tornado Publications.

Owusu, Maxwell, 1979. 'Politics Without Parties: Reflections on the Union Government Proposals in Ghana', *African Studies Review*, 22 (April), pp. 89–108.

Ozanne, Paul C., 1971. 'Ghana' in P. L. Shinnie (ed.), *The African Iron Age*, Oxford, Clarendon Press, pp. 36–65.

Pagni, Lucien, 1985. 'Ghana: The Success of the Revolution Depends on the Success of the Economy', *The Courier*, No. 90, March–April, pp. 29–40.

Peil, Margaret, 1973. 'Influence of Formal Education on Occupational Choice', *Canadian Journal of African Studies*, 7 (2), pp. 197–214.

Pinkney, Roger, 1972. *Ghana Under Military Rule*. London, Methuen.

Pluto/Maspéro, 1983. *World View 1983: an Economic and Geopolitical Yearbook*. London and Paris, Pluto and Maspéro.

Posnansky, Merrick, 1982. 'Ghana' in M. Posnansky and C. Ehret (eds), *Towards an Archaeological and Linguistic Interpretation of African History*, Berkeley, University of California Press.

——, 1984. 'Ghana's Earliest Agricultural Societies', in J. Desmond Clark and Steven A. Brant (eds), *From Hunters to Farmers: The Causes and Consequences of Food Production in Africa*, Berkeley, University of California Press.

Pratt, Cranford, 1976. *The Critical Phase in Tanzania 1945–1968: Nyerere and the Emergence of a Socialist Strategy*. Cambridge, Cambridge University Press.

Pratt, Larry, 1977. 'The State and Province-building: Alberta's Development Strategy', pp. 133–62 in Leo Panitch (ed.), *The Canadian State: Political Economy and Political Power*, Toronto, University of Toronto Press.

Price, J. H., 1967. *Political Institutions of West Africa*. London, Hutchinson Educational.

Price, Robert M., 1975. *Society and Bureaucracy in Contemporary Ghana*. Berkeley, University of California.

——, 1984. 'Neo-Colonialism and Ghana's Economic Decline: A Critical Assessment', *Canadian Journal of African Studies*, 18 (1), pp. 163–93.

Provisional National Defence Council, 1981. 'Provisional National Defence Council (Establishment) Proclamation, 1981', Ghana Publishing Corporation, Accra—Tema, GPC/A169/500/83 (effective 31 December 1981).

——, 1984. *Ghana, Two Years of Transformation: 1982–83*. Accra, Ghana, Information Services Department.

Rathbone, Richard, 1968. 'The Transfer of Power in Ghana', Ph.D. thesis, University of London.

— , 1978. 'Ghana', in *West African States: Failure and Promise*, John Dunn (ed.), Cambridge, Cambridge University Press.

Rattray, R. S., 1923. *Ashanti*. Oxford, Clarendon Press.

Rawlings, Flt.-Lt. J. J., 31 December 1982. 'We Will Resist Injustice', Speech on GBC, Accra, Ghana Press Release No. 4/82.

— , 28 August 1983. 'Discipline and Productivity', Accra, Information Services Department.

Ray, Donald I., 1979. *Administering Rural Development: The Role of Settlement Schemes in Zambia* Toronto, University of Toronto Ph.D.

— 1983. 'Solving the Food Crisis in Northern Ghana: The Potential of Traditional Rulers as a Policy Instrument', Boston, African Studies Association (USA).

— , Kense, François J., & Gavua, Kodzo, 1984. 'The PNDC, Traditional Structures and Development in Daboya, Ghana', Antigonish, Canadian Association of African Studies.

Reeck, Darrell, 1976. 'The Castle and the Umbrella: Some Religious Dimensions of Kwame Nkrumah's Religious Leadership in Ghana', *Africa Today*, 3 (4), pp. 7–27.

Reynolds, Edward, 1975. 'Economic Imperialism: The Case of the Gold Coast', *Journal of Economic History*, 35 (1), pp. 94–116.

Robinson, Cedric J., 1983. *Black Marxism: The Making of the Black Radical Tradition*. London, Zed Books.

Rothchild, Donald, 1980. 'Military Regime Performance: An Appraisal of the Ghana Experience, 1972–78', *Comparative Politics*, 12 (4), pp. 459–79.

— , 1985. 'The Rawlings Revolution in Ghana: Pragmatism with Populist Rhetoric', *CSIS Africa Notes*, Washington, Georgetown University Center for Strategic and International Studies, 42 (May 2), pp. 1–6.

— , & Gyimah-Boadi, E., 1981. 'Ghana's return to civilian rule', *Africa Today*, 28 (1), pp. 3–16.

Saaka, Yakubu, 1977. 'Local Government as an Agent of Secularization: the Case of the Gonja District of Northern Ghana', Ph.D. dissertation, Case Western Reserve University.

Sandbrook, Richard, & Arn, Jack, 1977. *The Labouring Poor and Urban Class Formation: The Case of Greater Accra*. Montreal, Centre for Developing-Area Studies, McGill University, Occasional Monograph Series, No. 12.

— , — , 1980. 'On the Theory and Practice of the Labouring Poor: A Reply to Peter Gutkind', *International Journal of African Historical Studies*, 13 (3), pp. 517–34.

Sathyamurthy, T. V., 1972. 'Politics of Independent Africa: A Review Article', *Africa Today*, **19** (3), pp. 64–72.

Saul, John S., 1979a. 'The Dialectics of Class and Tribe', *Studies in Political Economy*, No. 1 (Spring), pp. 1–42.

—— 1979b, *The State and Revolution in Eastern Africa*, New York, Monthly Review Press.

——, & Arrighi, Giovanni, 1973. *Essays on the Political Economy of Africa*. New York, Monthly Review Press.

Segal, R., 1962. 'Introduction', in *Portugal in Africa*, J. Duffy (ed.), Harmondsworth, Penguin.

Seton-Watson, Hugh, 1980. 'Aftermaths of Empire', *Journal of Contemporary History* (Britain), **15** (1), pp. 197–208.

Shaloff, Stanley, 1972. 'Press Controls and Sedition Proceedings in the Gold Coast, 1933–39', *African Affairs* (Britain), **71** (284), pp. 241–63.

Sheikh, Ahmed, 1972, 'Comparative Study of the Soviet and Third World Political Systems', *Political Science Review* (India), **11** (4), pp. 273–99.

Shinnie, P. L., (ed.), 1971. *The African Iron Age*. Oxford, Clarendon Press.

——, & Kense, F. J. (forthcoming), *Final Report on Excavations at Daboya, Ghana: 1978–1983*, Department of Archaeology, University of Calgary (forthcoming).

——, & Ozanne, P., 1962. 'Excavations at Yendi Dabari', *Transactions of the Historical Society in Ghana*, **6**, pp. 87–118.

Silver, Jim, 1978. 'Class Strugles in Ghana's Mining Industry', *Review of African Political Economy*, **12**, pp. 67–86.

Smart, M. Neff, 1975. 'School/Community Newspapers: An Experiment in Rural Ghana', *Rural Africana*, **27** (Spring), pp. 53–8.

Smertin, I. U., 1982. 'Lessons of Development', *Aziia: Afrika Segondnia* (USSR) (3), pp. 17–19.

South, 1984. 'Ghana: Republic of Ghana', October 1984.

Southall, Roger, & Kaufert, Joseph M., 1974. 'Converging Models of University Developments: Ghana and East Africa', *Canadian Journal of African Studies* **8** (3), pp. 607–28.

Spitzer, Leo, & Denzer, LaRay, 1973. 'I.T.A. Wallace-Johnson and the West African Youth League', *International Journal of African Historical Studies*, **6** (3), pp. 413–52 and **6** (4), pp. 565–601.

Stevens, Chris, 1974. 'In Search of the Economic Kingdom: The Development of Economic Relations between Ghana and the USSR', *Journal of Developing Areas*, **9** (1), pp. 3–26.

Struthers, John, 1981. 'Inflation in Ghana (1966–78): A Perspective on the Monetarist v. Structuralist Debate', *Development and Change*, **12** (2), pp. 177–214.

Sutton-Jones, Stuart, 1979. 'Ghana: Yesterday's Men vs the Day Before Yesterday's Men?', *Africa*, March, pp. 10–15.

Szajkowski, Bogdan (ed.), 1981. *Marxist Governments: A World Survey: Vol. 1 Albania–The Congo; Vol. 2 Cuba–Mongolia; Vol. 3 Mozambique–Yugoslavia*. New York, St. Martin's Press.

—— , 1982. *The Establishment of Marxist Regimes*. London, Butterworth Scientific.

Szule, Ewa, 1980. 'Production Cooperatives in Ghana—The Komenda Region', *History of Agriculture*, **2** (2), pp. 68–90.

Tarimo, Anatoli N. A., 1972. 'A discussion on Socialism—the Ghana case', *Taamuli* (Tanzania), **3** (1), pp. 36–42.

Thomas, Roger G., 1975. 'Education in Northern Ghana, 1906–1940: A Study in Colonial Paradox', *International Journal of African Historical Studies*, **7** (3), pp. 427–67.

Thompson, W. Scott, 1969. *Ghana's Foreign Policy. 1957–1966*, Princeton, Princeton University Press.

—— , 1973. 'The Communist Powers and Africa', *Orbis*, **16** (4), pp. 1066–9.

—— , 1977. 'Toward a Communist International System', *Orbis*, **20** (4), pp. 841–5.

Torbjornsson, Peter, 1984. 'Fidel on Nicaragua, El Salvador and the U.S. Threat', *The Guardian* (New York), 26 December, p. 56.

Trachtman, Lester N., 1961. 'Ghanaian Labour Legislation Since Independence', *Labour Law Journal*, **12** (June), pp. 548–54.

Tunteng, P. Kiven., 1974. 'George Padmore's Impact on Africa: A Critical Appraisal', *Phylon*, **35** (1), pp. 33–4.

Twumasi, Yaw, 1980. 'The Newspaper Press and Political Leadership in Developing Nations: The Case of Ghana 1964 to 1978', *Gazette* (Netherlands), **26** (1), pp. 1–16.

UNICEF/World Health Organization, 1977. *Report for the 1977 UNICEF/ WHO Joint Committee on health policy*. Geneva, UNICEF/WHO.

US Department of Commerce, Bureau of the Census, 1977. *Ghana*. Country Demographic Profiles ISP-DP-5.

US Department of State, May 1978. *Ghana: Background Notes*.

United States of America, State Department, 1985. *Country Reports on Human Rights Practices for 1984*.

Valpy, Michael, 1985. 'African Heads of State Seek a Common Front on Foreign Debt Crisis', *Globe and Mail*, 18 July.

Vercruijsse, E., 1979. 'Class Formation in the Peasant Economy of Southern Ghana', *Review of African Political Economy*, **15/16**, pp. 93–104.

Walker, Sandra, 1983. 'A Revolution That Isn't Happening', *The Guardian* (New York), 21 December.

Wallerstein, Immanuel, 1974. *The Modern World-System I: Capitalist Agriculture and the Origins of the European World-Economy in the Sixteenth Century*. New York and London, Academic Press.

Ward, W. E. F., 1948. *A History of the Gold Coast*. London, Allen & Unwin.

—— , 1966. *History of Ghana*. London, Allen & Unwin.

Weis, Lois, 1979. 'Education and the reproduction of inequality: the case of Ghana', *Comparative Education Review*, **23** (February), pp. 41–79.

Welch, Claude E., 1972. 'Praetorianism in Commonwealth West Africa', *Journal of Modern African Studies*, **10** (2), pp. 203–22.

—— , 1983. 'Military disengagement from politics: lesson from West Africa (Ghana, Nigeria and Sierra Leone)', *Armed Forces and Society*, **9** (Summer), pp. 541–54.

Werlin, Herbert H., 1973. 'The Consequences of Corruption: The Ghanaian Experience', *Political Science Quarterly*, **88** (1), pp. 71–85.

West Africa, 1981. 'Spotlight on Ghana', 11 May, pp. 1035–42.

Wilks, Ivor, 1975. *Asante in the Nineteenth Century*. Cambridge, Cambridge University Press.

—— , 1976. 'The Mossi and Akan States 1500–1880', in *History of West Africa*, Vol. 1, 2nd edn., Harlow, J. F. A. Ajayi and Michael Crowder (eds), pp. 413–55, Essex, Longman.

World Bank, 1984. *World Development Report 1984*. Oxford, Oxford University Press.

World Marxist Review, 1975. 'Brief information on Communist and Workers' parties', **18** (6), pp. 38–41.

Woronoff, Jon, 1973. 'Nkrumah—the Prophet Risen', *Worldview*, **16** (3), pp. 32–6.

Yeebo, Zaya, 1985. 'Ghana: Defence Committees and the Class Struggle', *Review of African Political Economy*, No. 32, pp. 64–72.

Zeff, Eleanor E., 1981. 'New Directions in Understanding Military and Civilian Regimes in Ghana', *African Studies Review*, **24** (1), pp. 49–72.

Newspapers

Africa Confidential (London).
Concord Weekly (London and Lagos).

Daily Graphic (Accra).
Ghana News (Washington DC).
Ghanaian Times (Accra).
Legon Observer (Legon, Accra).
People's Daily Graphic (Accra).
The Post (Ghana Information Services, Accra).
Weekly Spectator (Accra).
West Africa (London)
Workers' Banner (Accra).

Index